HUNGRY FOR GOD

An incredible book designed for all those who desire a deeper and more meaningful relationship with God

Published by Terry J. Boyle
Copyright © Terry John Boyle 2023.

Unless otherwise noted, all scripture quotations are taken from the Holy Bible, New King James Version Copyright © 1979, 1980, 1982 by Thomas Nelson, Inc.

All rights reserved. No part of this book may be reproduced in any form, stored in a retrieval system, or transmitted in any form by any means—electronic, mechanical, photocopy, recording or otherwise—without the prior written permission of the publisher, except as provided by Australian copyright law.

Words in capitals, or in bold or italics are the emphases of the author Terry Boyle – terryjohnboyle@bigpond.com

Cover & typeset by Carl Butel at Deep Image – carl@deepimage.net.au

Cataloguing-in-Publication data is available from the National Library of Australia.

ISBN 978-0-646-88234-5
eBook ISBN 978-0-646-88235-2

Disclaimer

As a result of this book, the author and publisher take no responsibility if the reader decides to fast for 40 days. They take no blame if someone does fast and has medical issues, physically or mentally.
Fasting can be dangerous and may affect a person's well-being.
This book is designed to create a hunger and thirst for God and is not a recommendation for fasting.

Acknowledgments

I thank my wife, Caroline, for her incredible love and support, especially during this time of fasting and prayer. Thank you to our children Amanda, Felicity, Andrew, Sharon, and their spouses and children for their encouragement.

To our daughter Amanda Butel, who is always supportive with her wise suggestions and input into the book. Especially to her husband, Carl Butel, for his fantastic cover design, internal layout, and getting the book ready for the publisher.

To my son Andrew, now a Baptist minister, for his scrutiny, wise input, and suggestions for the book.

To the late John and Coby Pasterkamp for inviting us to come and establish a Bible College in Port Moresby.

For all those in Papua New Guinea who have contributed in some way over the years. Especially to all those students and staff involved in the Bible College during our time in PNG. To the carpenters dedicated to building the College, Tom Kuipers, Steven DeBoer, and Ian Wylie. To expatriates for their support, Mike and Elizabeth Worthing, Peter and Gloria Steinbring, Bill and Mary McIntyre, Ruth George, "House of Ruth" (Nee Vaughn), Maria Von Trapp.

To those involved in ministry and administration – Auntie Rose, Ruth, Glenys McDonald, Hank, and Leni Vanderstein. (some above have passed on to be with the Lord.)

I still have contact with Pinaria Sialis, Charles Lapa, Gabriel Pepson, Unga and Lena Wangatua, Jack Pukari, Dr. Nicholas Mann, Thomas Palet, Solomon Vele, and many others.

Thanks to all those saints in the church in Lismore, where we spent 21 years as the senior pastor and chairman of Summerland Christian College.

To all church leaders for their input into our lives, especially those ministers in A2A (Acts 2 Alliance) and other Christian friends in Australia and overseas who have impacted our lives in some way for many years.

We are now enjoying our twilight years retired on the Gold Coast in Queensland, Australia.

CONTENTS

Preface	7
Introduction	9
Past struggles to fast and pray	11
The timing is so important	15
A longing for more of God	19
The Bread of Life	25
The first day	29
Perfect peace of mind	35
Say "No" to a spirit of fear	43
Striving together with one mind	49
Dealing with rogue thoughts	55
Did you find a religion or a friend?	61
Grace precedes faith	67
Activate your faith	71
Want God wants in every church	77
Equipped for ministry	83
The dealings of God	87
Waiting upon the Lord	95
The serpent, the Son, the cross	101
A zeal for the House of God	105
Do not fear the future	113
The message of the cross	119
Walking with God	123
Where are the spiritual Fathers?	129
What is the world coming to?	135
Know your identity in Christ	141
Was it worth it?	145
An amazing last day	151
In Honour of those now with the Lord	157

Photos - see page 156

1. Author, after a 40-day fast
2. Author and family in PNG
3. Group of Bible College students
   (John Pasterkamp on left, Terry Boyle on right)
4. College Classroom
5. Port Moresby Church crowd
6. Traditional welcome after 40 years

Preface

In my last book, "Enjoying Your Twilight Years," I briefly mentioned that while I was on the mission field in PNG, I felt this hunger and thirst for God. I believe the Holy Spirit led me to fast and pray. It was not my original intention, but I ended up fasting for 40 days.

I had kept a daily journal and said in passing, "I could write another book on the insights and revelations that came to me during that time." So, I thought I had better check my journals. After scanning them, I was sure I had enough inspirational, exciting, relevant, and thought-provoking material to format into another book.

However, I had a problem. I would have liked to have asked someone to write a foreword for this book as I have done with my last two books.

But these 40 days of fasting and prayer were some 40 years ago. It would be unfair to expect someone today to read and authenticate the manuscript. The only person who could fully know about this was Caroline, my wife.

So, instead of a foreword, I have included several photos to validate this remarkable time.

Hungry For God

Introduction

Sometimes, God calls us back into a more intimate relationship with Him. I was feeling this while we were on the mission field in PNG. I was longing for a fresh encounter with God. I decided to fast and pray. Apart from the leading of the Holy Spirit, several factors caused me to make that decision. The fast unintentionally lasted for 40 days.

I had been invited to Papua New Guinea to establish a Bible College to train national leaders. It was exciting as all this happened as God poured out His Holy Spirit. We were experiencing a revival in PNG, and many people turned to Christ. There were miracles of healing and deliverance. The local church, attached to the Bible College, grew from around 120 to over 500 in a few years.

The first four chapters establish a background leading up to the start of my fast. In chapter five, I begin with day one, taking daily extracts from my journal during the 40-day fast. Although this happened some 40 years ago, they are still relevant today. Some of the entries were a bit sketchy, but I will do my best with what I can decipher. Anyway, here it is. I hope you enjoy it.

Chapter 1
Past struggles to fast and pray

I had struggled in the past to fast and pray. Some of those memories were not very pleasant.

As a new Christian, I knew nothing about fasting other than it was in the Bible; Jesus did it, condoned it, and the Apostles practiced it.

Almost a disaster

The very first time I fasted was almost a disaster. I decided to fast for three days and nights. I thought fasting meant total abstinence from food and water. Nobody told me I was to drink water. I became dehydrated and felt so weak and miserable.

Yet by the grace of I felt a little closer to God. I may never have fasted again if I had not felt that closeness.

A little bit at a time

After that initial experience, I decided to fast a little bit at a time. I would regularly miss a meal, usually lunch, but I realised that many busy working people would often skip lunch.

I then started to do a full day once a week, and I would do this for about a month, have a break, and then continue for another month. Although this focused more on the discipline of fasting, I felt closer to God. Maybe I had a clear conscience because I was genuinely trying to improve my relationship with God.

Not defying the grace of God

I know this seems to deny the grace of God and borders on self-righteous works, but I felt good about it at the time. It was all a part of God preparing me for future ministry.

I love God's grace and understand more about God's grace because of this time. I intend to write a book on my scriptural revelation, experience, and understanding of the grace of God and how I found freedom from religiosity. It will be a real eye-opener for some people. But at this time, I was committed to seeking God this way.

A miserable ministry team

Around this time, I joined the ministry team of a thriving Charismatic Church in Melbourne under the leadership of the late Hal Oxley.

They were exciting days; God was pouring out His Spirit, and many turned to Christ, and many were healed and delivered during those days.

Hal decided we should all fast and pray as a ministry team for a week. Sunday was the last day of our week of fasting. We all sat on the platform in front of the people. We had not told anyone that we were fasting.

We all looked so miserable and sick that some people thought we all had a dose of the flu. After the service, several people came and asked us if we were okay as they were concerned for our welfare.

None of us were excited about our week of fasting and felt uninspired while fasting. But the week after we finished, we all seemed to have the energy to press into God.

As a result, we were encouraged by the fresh insights and revelations we shared. Some of these filtered down to benefit the church.

I can smell food

In those days, Hal asked me to take charge of a healing meeting with Allan Meyer. Allan was the youth pastor then (now Dr. Allan Meyer, founder of Lifekey Ministries.) We had agreed to fast for a few days for these meetings held in the church every Tuesday morning.

My office was next to Allan's, and on one of those fasting days, I could smell the wonderful aroma of food. I crept out of my office and quietly opened his door. I could not believe what I saw. Allan was sitting at his desk feasting on fish and chips. I was stunned. I said, "I thought we were fasting." He was shocked that he was sprung and replied, "I'm sorry, please forgive me. I was walking past this fish and chip shop; I was so hungry, I could not help myself." What could I do? I had to forgive him, so I helped him finish the fish and chips.

Miracles by the grace of God

Despite failing to finish that fast, many people were still saved, healed, and delivered in those healing meetings.

I will never forget one morning a charismatic catholic lady came with her 12-year-old son, who had been diagnosed with an inoperable brain tumour and only had about three months to live. The mother was desperate, so we anointed him with oil and prayed for his healing. About three months later, the lady rang me and said, "Do you remember praying for my son with the brain tumour." I hesitantly said, "Yes, I do," hoping she would not tell me that he had died. She said, "After you prayed, he improved, and further scans revealed that the tumour had disappeared, and now he is back at school and leading a normal life." I was overwhelmed with emotion. The Lord had honoured that mother's faith.

Chapter 2

The timing is so important

With any prolonged fast, the timing is so important. I felt the timing was right for me to fast, pray, and seek God. Why did I think that way at the time?

Several factors dovetailed together, and apart from trying to quench my hunger and thirst for God, there was a manifold purpose to it all.

A time for change

The late John Pasterkamp, the founder of CLC in PNG, who had invited me to come and establish a Bible College, had decided it was time to move on and leave me in charge of the work. John and Coby were going to Japan to pioneer a church in that nation.

We had established the Bible College over three years and felt we had accomplished what God had called us to, but now we faced a new challenge. (We ended up staying another three years).

Apart from the desire to seek God to quench the hunger and thirst for more of Him, I needed to find His wisdom to face not only this new responsibility but also for direction and guidance for future ministry when we were due to return to Australia.

I decided to give it a go

I thought this would be the best course of action at the time. So, I decided to give it a week to see what would happen.

I became excited in my spirit by the possible outcomes of a time of fasting and prayer, but my mind did not share the same excitement. The thought of missing out on food left me feeling flat. But my hunger for more of God overruled my feelings. I was committed to giving it a go.

After my daily routine, which I will outline later, the highlight of my day was to hop in our old Dyna Bus and head for a secluded spot I had found in the hills just outside of the city of Port Moresby to pray and meditate on the Word.

I would usually return home just as it was getting dark. Caroline was pregnant with Sharon, and the smell of some foods made her feel sick when she was cooking. I would offer to stir the food to help her get away from it, and I would inhale the smell. Maybe I was tormenting myself, but strangely enough, I found it helpful.

But I restrained myself and did not eat anything for forty days. I would drink plenty of water and a little fruit juice, sometimes with a dash of lemonade and the odd cup of Milo.

The timing is so important

As you can imagine, I lost a lot of weight *(see photo below)* but could still maintain a regular working routine.

I have not felt to share about this time of fasting and prayer until now, some 40 years later. I had thought people would think I was boasting because I had fasted for 40 days, and they would label me as being proud or a religious freak, and they would probably not believe me anyway. So, for years, I have rarely spoken about it.

But now I am in my twilight years; I do not care what people think. Although I hardly ever fast these days, I look forward to sharing extracts from my journal daily with some added stories of many adventures related to this incredibly challenging and exciting time.

Chapter 3

A longing for more of God

Apart from the right timing to fast and pray, my primary motivation was to quench this insatiable hunger and thirst for more of God in my life and ministry. This scripture describes how I felt.

> *"As the deer pants for the water brooks, so pants my soul for you, O God. My soul thirsts for God for the living God. When shall I come and appear before God?" Psalm 42:1-2.*

A deer pants when it tires from running and wants to quench its thirst. The word pant in this context can be translated as 'longs' for God. I was longing for God. I longed for a connection with the living God. The writer asks, "When shall I appear before God?" Or we could interpret that as when will I encounter God? It was undoubtedly my goal.

Jesus said, *"Blessed are those who hunger and thirst for righteousness, for they shall be filled." Matthew 5:6.* Jesus said they SHALL be filled, not maybe filled. I was longing to be filled.

However, I did not want my desire to fast and pray to become a stumbling block to others. They may think they must do the same. I do not want people to set out for a 40-day fast to copy me after reading this book. Or some may brush this experience off and interpret it as mere self-righteous religious works.

Watch out for religious pride!

I am well aware of the danger of religious pride when fasting. Jesus refers to this in the Pharisee and the Tax Collector parable.

> *'Two men went up to the temple to pray. The Pharisee stood and prayed thus with himself, "God, I thank You that I am not like other men – extortioners, unjust, adulterers, or even as this tax collector. I fast twice a week; I give tithes of all I possess." And the tax collector, standing afar off, would not so much as raise his eyes to heaven but beat his breast, saying, "God be merciful to me, a sinner!" "I tell you, this man went down to his house justified rather than the other." Luke 18:10-14.*

Jesus was not impressed by the self-righteous religious list of works that the Pharisee was proud of, which included fasting as a justifiable means of getting a response from God. It is interesting to note that Jesus said he "Prayed thus with himself." It was as though his prayers were bouncing off the ceiling.

But Jesus commended the tax collector who cried out, "God be merciful to me, a sinner." Jesus said this man humbled himself and returned to his house more justified than the Pharisee. We are justified today through our faith in Jesus Christ, our Saviour, and not our self-righteous works.

Christianity is not a religion; it announces the end of all other religions. Religion has tried and failed to please God. Jesus became the once for all acceptable sacrifice for our sins through His death on the cross and His resurrection. Our faith in His finished work on the cross now justifies us, not our religious pride or self-righteous works, which may include fasting.

However, Jesus did not condemn the spiritual discipline of fasting; He encouraged us to seek Him in faith with our whole heart. It may include fasting and prayer for some particular need where we may need to experience a breakthrough.

Some Biblical examples

I found plenty of scriptural support for fasting. But I will cite a few from the New Testament. It is not an in-depth study on the subject, as there are plenty of books with details on how to fast and pray.

The scripture that first got my attention was how Jesus was led by the Holy Spirit into the wilderness to be tempted by the devil.

It says, *"When He had fasted for forty days and forty nights, afterward He was hungry." Matthew 4:2.*

No wonder Jesus was hungry after fasting for 40 days in the wilderness. You can imagine how harsh the conditions would have been for Him to survive. Jesus would have been starving, so the devil tempted him to turn stones into bread. If it had been me, I would have thought, why not? I have earned it and quickly turned a suitable stone into a nice fresh loaf of bread.

But Jesus knew it was a temptation and resisted by saying, *"It is written, Man shall not live by bread alone, but by every word that proceeds from the mouth of God." Matthew 4:4.* Jesus overcame temptation by saying, *"It is written,"* and would quote an appropriate scripture to overcome the temptation He was facing.

Jesus said to His disciples when He was teaching about fasting and prayer, do not be like the hypocrites who like to appear to everyone that they are fasting. Jesus was saying that fasting and prayer were not to be used to impress others.

> *"...do not appear to men to be fasting, but to your Father who is in the secret place; and your Father who sees in secret will reward you openly". Matthew 6:16-18.*

Jesus said if you do this quietly in secret. In other words, please do not make a show of it and boast about it. I am not writing this to encourage you to fast or to impress you but hopefully to help you and inspire you to seek God to quench the hunger and thirst in your heart.

The disciples and apostles also fasted and prayed at times; they usually did this to seek God for direction and guidance, like in the context below.

> *'As they ministered to the Lord and fasted, the Holy Spirit said, "Now separate to me Barnabas and Saul for the work to which I have called them." Then when they had fasted and prayed, they laid hands on them, they sent them away.' Acts 13:2-3.*

This time of fasting and prayer was in conjunction with leaders forming a group, which included prophets and the laying on of hands. On this particular occasion, to send them out on missionary journeys.

Hungry For God

Chapter 4

The Bread of Life

Jesus is the bread of life!

"I am the bread of life. He who comes to Me shall never hunger, and he who believes in Me shall never thirst." John 6:35.

I believe God wanted me to feast on the bread of life. It was the answer to my hunger and thirst for more of God. Although Jesus uses a spiritual metaphor, I felt He was saying His word would sustain me and become my food during fasting.

Jesus said, *"Man shall not live by bread alone, but by every word that proceeds out of the mouth of God." Matthew 4:4*

When Job was going through a hard time, he did not blame God and would feed upon his word for comfort and reassurance.

"I have treasured the words of His mouth more than my necessary food." Job 23:12.

I also felt the word of God would be my necessary food. That, of course, is not meant to be literal; you would never find me munching on a bible.

Feeding upon the Bread of Life does not subdue the hunger pangs for food. They still exist. I like my food. I try eating healthy, but I still enjoy going to McDonald's. Thankfully, there were none in PNG in those days.

Jesus, Moses, and Elijah

Apart from Jesus, I knew Moses and Elijah had fasted 40 days. Interestingly enough, they appeared together on the Mount of Transfiguration with Jesus.

"Jesus took Peter, James, and John, his brother, led them up on a high mountain by themselves; and He was transfigured before them. His face shone like the sun, and His clothes became as white as the light. And behold Moses and Elijah appeared to them, talking with Him". Matthew 17:1-3.

Wow, how incredible. I can understand spiritual giants like Moses and Elijah fasting for 40 days. I am certainly not in that league. But in the back of my mind, I wondered what it would be like to have that experience and if I could do it. Would God spectacularly manifest Himself for me?

On the last day of the fast, I was ready for anything, and something incredible happened. You will have to keep reading to find out what took place.

The significance of 40

The Bread of Life

By way of interest, 40 signifies new life, growth, transformation, and change, usually after a trial or test of faith.

My time of fasting and prayer was some 40 years ago. Why has it taken me so long to put something in print? The answer is complicated. For years, I thought it was not something to talk about, as you were to do it in humility and, if possible, in secret.

It is interesting to note that Psalm 40 (of all Psalms) seems to sum up the process of seeking God, how out of desperation, there is an apparent hunger and thirst for God. It portrays what will happen when we pray and seek the Lord. In despair, he takes us from where we are to establish ourselves and put a new song in our mouth.

Look at how it unfolds -

"I waited patiently for the Lord, and He inclined to me and heard my cry. He also brought me up out of a horrible pit, out of the miry clay, and set my feet upon a rock, and established my steps. He has put a new song in my mouth..." It is not about how we start but how we finish. The result is always worth it.

Some of the significant 40s in the Bible –

- It rained for 40 days and nights for the flood.
- Moses fasted 40 days and nights.
- The Israelites wandered for 40 years in the Wilderness.
- The Prophet Elijah journeyed 40 days to get to the Mountain of God.

- Jesus fasted 40 days and nights.
- Jesus ascended into Heaven 40 days after His resurrection.

How I will do the rest of the book

Starting in Chapter 5 - I will take extracts every day from my journal and add true stories related to the time I spent ministering with other lecturers and students in their home provinces. I will do this by fast-forwarding and rewinding at times to fit in these exciting stories to add interest and give the reader a greater understanding of the PNG culture and how God was pouring out His Spirit.

Chapter 5

The first day

Day 1 (Journal)

It was a Sunday, a typical hot, steamy Port Moresby day. I decided I would start today! We had a visiting speaker, Mygo, who was pastoring a church on the island of Daru near the mouth of the mighty Fly River.

Rewind for a moment - I will never forget when I went to Daru. I had been invited as the speaker by pastor Jack Laukepe to speak at an open-air crusade. When the plane landed on the tarmac before we disembarked, I saw an official-looking party lined up, ready to greet someone through the window. I told the person next to me, *"There must be some government VIP on the plane."* To my surprise, the VIP was me; it was to welcome me officially.

The churches had combined for the crusade, so the pastors and leaders had lined up to welcome me. I was the honoured guest. The campaign was incredible. It grew over the three nights from around 500 people to 2000. Many turned to Christ. Others were healed and delivered.

After the crusade, they took me up the Fly River in an open boat to minister to people who could not attend the campaign. We traveled all day, and despite wearing a hat, I got very sunburnt. It's hard to believe, but even some nationals got sunburnt.

We stopped at a remote village where a crowd had gathered. I preached with swollen, sunburnt lips, and we had a great response from the people. We overnighted and headed back the next day.

As we came out of the mouth of the Fly River, it was dark, and we hit something in the water and broke the shear pin on the propeller. Although the waves buffeted us, they replaced the shear pin and headed towards the lights of Daru in the distance.

When we arrived back, I was exhausted, sunburnt, and feeling deflated. I remember saying to the Lord, *"Why am I doing this?"* He replied, *"Because you love me, and I have chosen you."* I rolled over and went to sleep with a smile on my face.

Before I left to return to Port Moresby the next day, they put on a fantastic feast in my honour. It was a great buffet with all kinds of food, some I had not tasted before, like Crocodile, Shark, Turtle, and Deer meat. They were all caught locally.

Day 1 (Journal)

The first day

Mygo's message - She preached that morning: *"Reaching out to the lost with compassion for the poor and needy."* She used as her text Matthew 9:36.

"When Jesus saw the multitudes, He was moved with compassion for them because they were weary and scattered, like sheep having no shepherd."

Mygo quoted Kathryn Kuhlman, who had a tremendous healing ministry, saying, *"I have a love and a compassion for humanity; without it, I would immediately stop preaching."* I hope all preachers feel that way.

That afternoon, I rested around the house and the church grounds with my wife and family. Late that night, I spent some time in the Word. I felt the Lord was preparing me to renew my mind and that He would reveal ways to do it.

Day 2

Monday – Firstly, let me outline my daily routine.

Before I start making entries from my journal, most days looked something like the following. I do not want to keep repeating it. I will give you a general outline.

I would take our daughters Amanda and Felicity to an International School, drop them off before 8 a.m., and pick them up at 2 p.m. (Andrew was only five months old when we arrived in PNG, and Sharon was born in Port Moresby).

When I was rostered on to lecture in Bible College, I would spend the morning with the students. Otherwise, I would take my wife shopping, do odd jobs, or study. After picking the children up from school and dropping them back home, I would head out to pray in my secluded spot in the hills just outside Port Moresby.

I will continue to fast-forward and rewind as we go through my journal by adding some exciting and challenging stories, just like the one I told about my time in Daru because we had Mygo from Daru ministering that Sunday morning. Hopefully, these stories will bless and inspire you in your relationship with God.

Day 2 (Journal)

After taking lectures this morning, I concentrated on studying the renewing of the Mind.

> *"Do not be conformed to this world, but be transformed by the renewing of your mind, that you may prove what is that good, and acceptable, and perfect will of God." Romans 12:2.*

I had preached on this verse many times before. But the word 'transformed' seemed to jump out at me more than it had in the past. The Greek transformed can be translated as 'metamorphose,' like a caterpillar changing into a butterfly.

It seemed as though the Lord was challenging me to change from worldly thinking to Godly thinking and that He would show me how to go about it.

It was getting late. So, I decided to spend some time praying. As I prayed, the Lord reassured me that I was off to a great start. I seemed to be communicating with Him.

Hearing from God already

I was hearing from God already. I thought of the scripture in Daniel where he had been praying and fasting and seeking the Lord for three weeks until finally, an Angel came and said to him.

> *"Do not fear, Daniel, for from the FIRST DAY that you set your heart to understand and humble yourself before your God, your words were heard, and I have come because of your words." Daniel 10:12.*

Even though it took Daniel three weeks to break through in prayer because of spiritual resistance, God had heard his prayers from the very first day. I also felt I was being listened to from day one, which inspired me to continue.

Chapter 6

Perfect peace of mind

Day 3 (Journal)

Pastor David Muap, who is on staff as one of the national pastors, took lectures this morning. David and his wife Clara are a part of the team.

Rewind for a moment - I will never forget going with David to live in his village, Kontu, on the West coast of New Ireland, PNG. We were there for about ten days. I loved it.

The village was lovely, with palm trees around a beautiful coral lagoon. The beach was a mixture of pebbles and sand. At low tide, freshwater springs would ooze up where they had made pools for washing and collecting water. These springs were fed underground from the rugged mountain ranges and dense jungle behind the village.

The people were so gracious and looked after us. Some mornings, we woke up to find our breakfast sitting at the front door of our hut; it was usually a freshly cooked fish on a plate staring up at us or a cooked crab served with some rice.

I was fascinated by their traditional method of catching sharks. The Australian ABC was filming and producing a documentary called "The Shark Callers of Kontu" while we were there. In my first book, 'Unlocking Your Purpose,' I wrote about my time in the village and our attempt to catch a shark. I devoted the first chapter to 'Living with Shark Hunters' to this time, so I will not repeat it.

Day 3 (Journal)

I retreated to my research and started to think about having my mind renewed and fixed upon the Lord. But what does that mean from a scriptural point of view?

Peace of mind

> *"You will keep him in perfect peace, whose mind is stayed on you because he trusts in you. Trust in the Lord forever." Isaiah 26:3.*

This scripture does not refer to ordinary peace of mind, which usually depends on circumstances. It is a perfect peace of mind which can only come from God regardless of circumstances.

What is the secret to having our minds stayed or fixed upon the Lord? How do we do that?

Firstly, we must stay focused on the Lord and not be sidetracked by our circumstances. Secondly, we must continually put our faith and trust in the Lord to help us control our lives.

A vital scripture in the New Testament that complements the one we have just been looking at -

"Let the peace of God rule your hearts." Colossians 3:15.

This scripture refers to letting the peace of God be your umpire. Let His peace be the rule you live by. Let the referee blow the whistle if the rules are broken by you having no peace.

Stop and refocus. Fix your mind on the Lord and put your trust in Him until the peace of God takes control of your heart and mind.

Do not be double-minded

I asked the Lord to show me how to foster that peace of mind. A scripture in James came to mind.

> *"If any man lacks wisdom, let him ask of God, who gives to all liberally and without reproach, and it will be given him. But let him ask in faith, with no doubting, for he who doubts is like a wave of the sea driven and tossed by the wind. For let not that man suppose that he will receive anything from the Lord; he is a double-minded man, unstable in all his ways. James 1:5-8.*

I read it repeatedly and saw no room for doubting or being double-minded when asking God in faith for wisdom. A double-minded man is unstable in all his ways. That shocked me. I decided to investigate this further.

Being double-minded is not about having different opinions. We may all vary in our views on specific issues. But we should not waver when asking God for wisdom in difficult circumstances.

Day 4 (journal)

After taking lectures, I stayed home and studied. It is raining today; my bush track may be a little wet. So I decided to stay home all day.

Spiritual schizophrenia

As believers, we sometimes suffer from spiritual schizophrenia. Perhaps I am being a bit extreme, but I wanted to get your attention because I feel this is so important concerning where James mentions for believers not to be double-minded.

It would appear if we keep this passage in the context of the first five verses leading up to the above scripture, it would imply when we are going through trials and temptations and our faith is being tested that, we should ask God for wisdom to be able to survive whatever difficulty we are experiencing.

God promises to give us wisdom in abundance if we ask for it. Then comes the BUT. *"BUT let him ask in faith, with no doubting, for he who doubts is like a wave of the sea driven and tossed by the wind." Verse 6.*

When we doubt and become double-minded, like the wind and the waves, we will become unpredictable and changeable, nullifying our faith.

"For let not this man think he will suppose he will receive anything from the Lord from the Lord" verse 7. He is not likely to get an answer

from the Lord because of his wavering faith.

Unstable in all his ways

The real problem is that he is a double-minded man who has become unstable in all his ways. It means he has the potential to be confused, inconsistent, vacillating, unreliable, unpredictable, unsettled, and lacking in conviction when it comes to faith. *'He is a double-minded man, unstable in all his ways' James 1:8.* This is a very challenging and sobering thought.

The classic example goes back to the Garden of Eden. God had told Adam and Eve not to eat from the Tree of the Knowledge of good and evil. If they did, they would die. However, Satan came along and said to Eve, *"You will not surely die"….. "If you eat of it, you will become like God knowing good and evil"* Genesis 3:1-7.

Satan lied, and the seed of doubt took root, and they became double-minded, made a wrong decision, and ate the forbidden fruit.

Double-mindedness leads to instability and is a human weakness and an obstacle to our faith. It does not mean evil, but it hinders our faith, so we need to take control of our minds and deal with it.

Some steps to take

Here are a few steps to nip double-mindedness in the bud. We are all familiar with how our thoughts and feelings affect our behaviour.

1. Recognise rogue thoughts - thoughts that are unhelpful, negative, and destructive. Catch them before they do some damage.

2. Reframe your thoughts - to comply with the Word of God. Check and change them to bring peace to your mind and stabilise your emotions.

3. Re-connect with others – to modify or help you. Others can help balance our thoughts, feelings, and behaviour.

A form of spiritual warfare

Dealing with thoughts is a form of spiritual warfare.

> *"For the weapons of our warfare are not carnal but mighty in God for pulling down strongholds"* 2 Corinthians 10:4.

Where are those strongholds? Most of them are wrong thinking patterns that have developed in our minds.

Some years ago, this scripture became very real when I was in charge of a spiritual warfare meeting in Melbourne. A small group of us would pray for the nation of Australia to stand against the powers of darkness. At the time, I felt it was a bit nebulous and wondered if we were making any headway and if it was worthwhile until I had a dream.

In my dream, I was the prime minister's bodyguard and lived in a small house at the back of the lodge. As I looked out the window one day, I saw a swarm of black objects forming like planes coming over us. Two of these objects saw me as I looked and headed straight for me. I took my revolver and started shooting at them, but they kept coming at me. The next thing I knew was that the dream had become a reality as I was being choked and crushed. I could only whisper the name of Jesus, but as soon as I did, they immediately fled. I woke up shaken by the experience. My wife thought I was having a heart attack.

The Lord showed me clearly through this experience that powers of darkness were a reality and that natural weapons are not the answer, but spiritual weapons are, and the greatest weapon of all is the name of Jesus. The name of Jesus is above every name. *(Philippians 2:9-11)*.

The next part of the verse has more to do with the battle of the mind and the war that we need to wage in the area of our minds.

> *"Casting down arguments and every high thing that exalts itself against the knowledge of God, bringing every thought into captivity to the obedience of Christ." Verve 5.*

We need to focus on this until we get victory over our rogue thoughts and renew our minds to conform to the will of God.

Chapter 7
Say "No" to a spirit of fear

Day 5

Pastor Lenden Butuna took Lectures this morning. Lenden was our Bible College Dean for the first year of the College. He was visiting from Alotau, where he was pastoring a church.

Rewind for a moment - A few months ago, Lenden invited me to come and speak at a combined church camp with the Uniting Church. It turned out to be the adventure of a lifetime.

We left Alotau early in the morning and traveled a long way until we came to a river in the middle of a palm plantation. There was a big boat waiting for us. It was full of supplies and people. We headed downriver for a long time until we eventually came out to sea in a beautiful sheltered bay. We sailed across the bay and came to a headland where the bay flowed into the ocean. The camp would be held in a village at the base of this headland.

Several canoes had been out fishing and spreading their catch on a bamboo platform for us to see as we came ashore. I had never seen such a variety of fish that became part of the camp menu.

We were warmly welcomed and taken to our accommodation, an old classroom on top of the headland. The view was magnificent. We looked out to the open sea on one side and back down the bay we had just been on.

I woke up early the following day, and as I looked out to sea, I saw two giant Manta Rays scraping the bottom as they were feeding, then leaping in the air and rolling over to repeat the process. It was an incredible sight.

The camp meetings were great; several people were saved, healed, and delivered. The blessing of the Lord was evident to all. But all good things come to an end. It was hard to leave that beautiful spot.

Day 5 (Journal)

Just because your mind needs to be transformed and renewed does not mean something is drastically wrong with your mind; you are just a victim of a fallen world that does not think as God thinks.

I turned to Timothy and read, *"For God has not given us a spirit of fear, but of power and of love and of a sound mind.' 2 Timothy 1:7.*

If fear torments us, troubles our minds, and hinders our faith, it is probably a spirit of fear. We need to learn to say

"No" to a spirit of fear. It is certainly not from God, for He has not given us a spirit of fear but of power, love, and a sound mind.

In the original Greek, a 'sound mind' means having a disciplined, self-controlled mind. Therefore, we can discipline, control, and correct our unruly thoughts to align with the word of God. We should not allow ourselves to be ruled by thoughts that create fear instead of faith. We need to take control of our thoughts and not let them control us.

Paul is writing to young Timothy to tell him to stir up the gift within him by laying on Paul's hands and not being intimidated by a spirit of fear. *(Verse 6)*.

Prophecy can be a weapon of war

We can use a prophetic word over our lives to stir up the gift of God within us. We can even use prophecy as a weapon of war to contradict and nullify the devil's condemnation.

> *"This charge I commit to you, son Timothy, according to the prophecies previously made over you, that buy them you may wage the good warfare." 1 Timothy 1:18.*

When someone we respect lays hands on us for some reason to impart something or they prophesy over us, we should value that word, let it encourage us, and use it in warfare against the enemy.

Be an example to others

We should not let the devil or people intimidate us through

fear but stir up the gift of God within us despite criticism and intimidation and be an example to other believers. Sometimes, in the heat of the battle, we shrink back in fear instead of stepping out in faith.

Paul encourages Timothy not to let the fear of man hinder his faith and ministry. *"Let no one despise your youth, but be an example to the believers in word, in conduct, in love, in spirit, in faith, and in purity"* 1 Timothy 4:12.

We have the mind of Christ

I turned to a verse that had troubled me for some time. *"For who has known the mind of the Lord that he may instruct Him?" But we have the mind of Christ.* 1 Corinthians 2:16.

The first part of the verse is not a problem; it is a quote from Isaiah virtually saying no one has known the mind of the Lord and who can instruct Him. We can all say Amen to that. But then it almost contradicts itself by saying, *"But we have the mind of Christ."*

If we have the mind of Christ, why do we need to renew our minds and transform our thinking to bring our thoughts in line with the word of God?

Why am I praying and fasting to seek the Lord for direction if I already have the mind of Christ? If I have the mind of Christ, I may as well stop praying and fasting and go and have a big feed.

Then I felt the Lord pointed out that it said, 'we' have the mind of Christ, plural, or more than one, not me or you as an individual. It is a reference that relates more to the church or the whole body of Christ.

The wisdom of God in the message of the cross

Looking at the context leading up to this verse, I saw some things that began to give me more understanding.

The context goes back to 1 Corinthians 1:18, with Paul declaring, *'For the message of the cross is foolishness to those who are perishing, but to us who are being saved, it is the power of God.'*

He explains that *"Christ crucified to the Jews a stumbling block and to the Greeks foolishness" verse 23.*

It made no sense to the Jews that the Messiah would come and be crucified instead of reigning as a King (a stumbling block), and foolishness to the Greeks, who could see no wisdom for the Messiah to be crucified. (their focus was on wisdom).

As this passage continues through to 2 Corinthians 2:16, it becomes clear that this is all about comparing God's wisdom to man's wisdom.

Here is an outline of how it unfolds -

1. The wisdom of God stands in sharp contrast to the wisdom of man.
2. The wisdom from God was once hidden but is revealed now in Christ.

3. The mind of Christ is imparted to believers through the Spirit of God.

4. Those without the Spirit cannot understand the mind of Christ.

5. The mind of Christ gives believers the discernment they need in spiritual matters.

We need to see the big picture. I would summarise it this way. The wisdom of God is in the message of the cross, which seems like foolishness to the world.

To have the mind of Christ as believers means we understand the wisdom of the message of the cross. It is how God plans to seek and save the lost by reaching the world through the power of the cross and preaching the gospel. It is Something man has trouble understanding.

We also have the mind of Christ (plural) as the church or as the whole body of Christ. I would suggest we have a measure of the mind of Christ as individuals but with limitations.

Chapter 8

Striving together with one mind

Day 6 (Journal)

I Lectured again this morning, then took my wife Caroline shopping before picking up the children from school, taking them home, and heading for the hills.

As I study, I will examine the mind of Christ concerning believers striving together with one mind and in unity for the faith of the gospel.

Unity does not happen automatically. Keeping the unity of the Spirit is something we have to work at continually.

In one spirit, with one mind

The issue is not so much doctrine; it is being of one mind with one spirit to proclaim the gospel. The priority is to spread the gospel; to be effective and have an impact, we need to strive together as believers in Christ.

> *"Only let your conduct be worthy of the gospel of Christ, so that whether I come and see you or am absent, I may hear of your affairs, that you stand fast in one spirit, with one mind striving together for the faith of the gospel." Philippians 1:27.*

The word 'striving' in Greek has almost an aggressiveness to it. The connotation is one of 'wrestling' for it to protect and keep it. We need to work at being in unity by being of one spirit and one mind. How do we do this? We have to strive together, stop squabbling among ourselves, and stand together to maintain unity and avoid strife and divisions in the life of a particular church or among other churches.

What are we striving for? For the 'faith' of the gospel, it is not seeking to all have the same doctrine (although that would be nice). It is to maintain the unity of the faith that the gospel continues to impact our community. We should shine as lights in a dark world desperately needing the gospel.

What is the key to keeping the unity of the Spirit? We already have it: the Spirit. But the real problem is holding it. *"…endeavouring to keep the unity of the Spirit in the bond of peace…" Ephesians 4:3.*

Being bound together in the bond of peace is so important. We are to be at peace with one another, not at war. We are at war with the devil, and we need to strive together against the enemy.

A Major problem in PNG

I will call it denominational tribalism. It stems from the tribal 'one talk' system. People from certain areas stick together and support one another, but they sometimes are not so friendly to other clans. Traditionally, they will sometimes take up arms and fight one another.

Unfortunately, this kind of mentality has crept into the church. Denominations have become dominant in certain areas. For example, if a particular village has been traditionally a Lutheran area, they can oppose other denominations from entering their territory.

In PNG, this can become a significant problem. People are very focused on their particular area or denomination and have become narrow-minded in their attitude toward others. It means it is challenging for the church to be in unity and be of one mind and one spirit.

However, there are signs that this problem is beginning to change. Although most churches stick to their denominations for conferences, some are starting to combine.

Disunity and division

Disunity and division are some of the devil's tactics to try and destroy the effectiveness of the church and the spread of the gospel of the kingdom.

Jesus said, *"Every kingdom divided against itself is bought to desolation, and every city or house divided against itself will not stand"* Matthew 12:25.

Rewind for a moment - Before coming to PNG, we went

through a church split in Australia. The senior pastor at the time had to leave a magnificent property. We had just built an Auditorium, a Manse, a Bible College Dormitory, a Kitchen and Dining area, a Lecture Room, and an Office Block. It was all built on five acres of land in Melbourne. The rift was between the Senior Pastor and the Associate Pastor.

I was on the ministry team and had to decide who to follow. I stuck with the Senior pastor. I do not want to go into the details, but it was a terrible time for everyone. A lot of people were confused, hurt, and very disillusioned.

The church was around 500 strong; about 350 followed the Senior pastor, and 150 stayed with the Associate Minister. We started services again in a High School hall. Eventually, we purchased land, built an auditorium, and continued to see the church grow.

Much later, the church sold what they had built to a funeral director, purchased large acreage on Melbourne's outskirts, and built a big auditorium and Christian School. Today, the church has over 1000 members, with a Christian School of over 2000 students.

The beautiful property we had to vacate years before due to the church split was eventually bulldozed for a housing estate some years later.

How should we behave? (Journal)

One of the keys to striving together for the gospel's faith is how we conduct ourselves and behave as Christians.

Our crucial scripture begins with *"Only let your conduct be worthy of the gospel of Christ….." Philippians 1:27.*

Paul goes on in chapter two of Philippians to elaborate on how we should conduct ourselves. I will highlight a few verses as they are self-explanatory.

"Let nothing be done through selfish ambition or conceit, but in lowliness of mind let each esteem others better than himself. Let each of you look out not only for his own interests but also for the interests of others". Philippians 2:3-4. In its context, it encourages us to humble ourselves, not be selfish, but to consider others for unity.

"Do all things without complaining and disputing, that you may become blameless and harmless, children of God without fault in the midst of a crooked and perverse generation, among whom you shine as lights." Philippians 2:14.

Paul is now addressing how we conduct ourselves both within ourselves and as a witness to the world. The world observes the behaviour of Christians and looks for faults to criticise.

It is so important to strive together to maintain the unity of the Spirit. When we do, the gospel will impact our community more.

Day 7 (Journal)

Today is Saturday, a special day. I officiated at the wedding of Peter and Anne Singut, who are ex-students. They are a lovely couple, and it was a joy to conduct the service. It was a wonderful celebration.

Chapter 9

Dealing with rogue thoughts

Day 8 (Journal)

It is hard to believe that a week has gone by already. I am feeling good and ready to preach the word this morning.

Vagi Vele led the worship with tears streaming down his face; the anointing and presence of God was overwhelming this morning. Vagi and his wife Mary are a lovely couple, ex-students, and now on the ministry team. Their son Solomon and our son Andrew play a lot together around the church property.

I spoke on an aspect of spiritual warfare -

"The battle of the mind," using for my text, "For the weapons of our warfare are not carnal but mighty through God to the pulling down of strongholds; casting down arguments and every high thing that exalts itself against the knowledge of God. 2 Corinthians 10:4-5.

I was all fired up because I had been studying the theme of renewing the mind all week.

I was concentrating on pulling down strongholds in our minds that were deceptive and negative and a hindrance to our faith and how we need to rearrange our thoughts to obey the word of God rather than those unruly thoughts that want to control us.

At the end of my message, I started to pray and rebuke demonic strongholds in the Spirit. I had not given an alter call, but people began to manifest with strange noises; some were very loud. People were being set free, and strongholds were crumbling. So, I kept praying and rebuking the enemy.

When things began to subside, I noticed a crowd had gathered around the church's perimeter. People walking past and those living nearby heard the noise and came to investigate. Later, there were many testimonies from people who had been set free of all sorts of bondages.

After church, I spent the rest of the day resting and spending some time with my family.

Day 9 (Journal)

After my usual morning routine and lecturing, I headed for the hills again with this scripture on my mind.

"For as he thinks in his heart so is he" Proverbs 23:7. Or as I had preached it, *"As a man thinks so he is."* Our thoughts are the seeds that shape our lives.

I have already established how important the mind is concerning our thoughts, but now, examining this verse, it is clear that our thinking is connected to our heart. In its context, this verse is about someone saying something to please you, but their heart is not with you. They welcome and invite you to their table but are treacherous and deceptive. It is why the verse tells us to avoid such a person.

Spiritual discernment

It led me to look at our need for spiritual discernment. I was familiar with the verse that mentions one of the nine gifts of the Spirit being *"Discerning of spirits,"* as in 1 Corinthians 12:10.

It means understanding or knowing something through the Holy Spirit's power. It is the ability to perceive the true character of people and the source of demonic manifestations. Some of these would be associated with spirits like pride, greed, lust, envy, gluttony, wrath, infirmities, and slothfulness, to mention a few. Demons seem more inclined to lose their grip on people when identified, named, and exposed.

Rewind for a moment - I will never forget one of my first encounters with a demon some years before coming to PNG. I was preaching in a small church in Australia. I was about to give an altar call, and a woman stood up and said in a guttural voice, "I hate your preaching." It shocked me and the congregation, but I was curious to know why. So realising a demon was manifesting, I told her, "Tell me why?" She put her hands over her ears and, in this weird voice, said, "Too much truth; I can't stand the truth." So I commanded the spirit in the name of Jesus to come out.

Back to my Journal - There is also the ability to discern someone's spirit or heart as to what they are thinking. "But when Jesus perceived (discerned) their thoughts, He answered and said to them, *"Why are you reasoning in your hearts."* Luke 5:22.

Nowadays, there is so much deception in the world we need the discerning of spirits. May God help us to exercise this gift.

Seven ways we can grow in this gift –

1. Realise Satan is out to deceive us
2. There can be false prophets and teachers
3. Test the spirits to see if they are from God
4. Do not believe everything you hear
5. Be led by the Holy Spirit
6. Allow the Word of God to help you discern
7. Seek God for the gift of discernment

Rewind for a moment - I was in a meeting worshipping the Lord in the front row and sensed someone standing before me. When I opened my eyes, a young lady I had never seen before looked up at me. She said, "I am the angel grace out of the book of revelation, and I have a message for your church."

I said, "No, you're not, now go and sit down."

Thankfully, she did, then she disappeared before the end of the meeting. I discerned that she was a false prophet. How did I do that? By automatically going through the above list in my mind in a split second. The one that stood out was when she said she was the angel Grace from the Book of Revelation. I am not aware of any such angel.

Hungry For God

Chapter 10

Did you find a religion or a friend?

Day 10 (Journal)

I feel good from a physical point of view; everything seems normal. I had a bowel movement, which surprised me, seeing I have had nothing to eat for the last nine days. I'm feeling good and looking forward to today.

We have Pastor John Ollis, the vice Principal of the Commonwealth Bible College (AOG) in Sydney, taking lectures this morning.

In my study time up until now, the Lord has been showing me things related to renewing the mind. But now, there seems to be a shift from this emphasis to my relationship with God.

You found a friend

The Lord reminded me that when I became a Christian, I did

not find a religion; I found a friend. *"There is a friend who sticks closer than a brother." Proverbs 18:24.* For Christians today, that friend is our Lord Jesus Christ.

How can that be? To find the answer, we have to go back to Abraham, who was called a friend of God. We are talking about Almighty God, the creator of heaven and earth. Can this awesome God be a friend to human beings?

Several scriptures refer to Abraham as a friend of God. What does that mean?

"Are you not our God who drove out the inhabitants of this land before Your people Israel, and gave it to the descendants of Abraham Your FRIEND forever?" 2 Chronicles 20:7.

"And the scripture was fulfilled which says, Abraham believed God, and it was accounted to him for righteousness. And he was called the FRIEND of God". James 2:23.

Why was he called the friend of God? Before we try and find an answer, it is interesting to look at his background. It would seem he had no relationship with God before God called him.

Abraham did not find a religion – he found a friend

It would appear that Abraham had an ungodly religious background. He was born and raised in Ur of the Chaldees, where they served other gods and worshiped idols.

"....Your fathers, including Terah, the father of Abraham and the

father of Nahor, dwelt on the other side of the River in old times; and they served other gods. Then I took your father Abraham from the other side of the River and led him throughout all the land of Canaan". Joshua 24:2-3.

Abraham had a religious background steeped in idol worship. No wonder when God called Abraham in Genesis 12:1, He said, *"Get out of your country, from your family and your father's house to a land that I will show you."* He had to leave everything behind, including his religious ways.

What a contrast from worshiping other gods and idols of wood and stone to serving a living God he could communicate with and become His friend.

Day 11 (Journal)

A new fasting record today. I have never fasted for longer than ten days. John Ollis continues with lectures again today. I will continue my study of a friend of God from home.

What does it mean to be a friend to someone? It is to have affection for them or mutual love and respect for them; it is to be on good terms with them and enjoy their company. How, then, did Abraham qualify to be a friend of God? He got off to a great start with God because he believed and obeyed God.

"Abraham believed God, and it was accounted to him for righteousness." Romans 4:3.

How can God be my friend?

What about us? We all come from different backgrounds,

some religious and some not, but we all had one thing in common: we were all lost in sin.

"For all have sinned and fall short of the glory of God." Romans 3:23.

But of course, the good news is that *"God so loved the world that He gave His only begotten Son, that whoever believes in Him should not perish but have eternal life." John 3:16.*

Did you notice that *"Whoever believes in Him?"* Abraham believed and laid a foundation for others to believe and, therefore, have the potential to have God as their friend.

How does that work for us as Christians today? How can we possibly be connected to Abraham? We are through his seed, which is a reference to Christ.

The seed of Abraham

Because of Abraham and his seed (Christ), God can be my friend and your friend. *"So then those who are of faith are blessed with believing Abraham." Galatians 3:9.*

It gets better, so let me clarify with a few more verses, *"Now to Abraham and his SEED were the promises made. He does not say, and to seeds, as of many, but as of one, and to your SEED, who is CHRIST. And if you are CHRIST'S, then you are Abraham's SEED and heirs according to the promise." Galatians 3:16 and 29.*

As Christians, we are Abraham's seed in Christ and inherit the promises of God by faith in Christ. We are no longer under the law. We have been liberated from the bondage of religion by the grace of God to live by faith. Therefore, we are justified in calling God our friend because of Christ.

We are not worshipping idols and gods made out of wood or stone. The demands of manufactured religious laws and regulations do not bind us. We are now relating to a God who is our friend.

When we became Christians, we did not find a religion. We found a friend. His name is Jesus!

He is someone we can relate to, walk with, and talk to, just like the words of the chorus of the old Hymn – 'I serve a risen Saviour.'

> He lives, He lives
>
> Christ Jesus lives today
>
> He walks with me and talks with me,
>
> along life's narrow way,
>
> He lives, He lives,
>
> Salvation to impart,
>
> You ask me how I know he lives,
>
> He lives within my heart.

Hungry For God

Chapter 11

Grace comes before faith

Day 12 (Journal)

John Ollis is continuing with lectures today.

Becoming a Christian depends on God's grace and our faith in Christ, not legalistic religious practices.

Grace comes first

> *"For by grace, you have been saved through faith, and that not of yourselves, it is the gift of God, not of works, lest anyone should boast." Ephesians 2:8-9.*

We see grace and faith working together to secure our salvation. But grace comes before faith. Without grace, we would not be able to exercise faith in Christ. We do not get to heaven by our good works. The only people in heaven will be sinners saved by grace, those who have put their faith in Christ.

By the grace of God, Abraham was chosen, not because

of his religious background, where he was serving other gods. Why was he selected in the first place? God saw something in him and extended His grace, and he responded in faith.

The Bible also mentions that God would judge and destroy the world with a flood in a wicked world. But *"Noah found grace in the eyes of the Lord." Genesis 6:8.* Although we deserve judgment today, we have found grace because of Christ.

Religious practices do not help Christians and the church. The church is in the business of proclaiming the gospel. God is not impressed by legalistic rules and liturgy. As I heard one preacher say, He is not looking for "Bells, smells, incense and nonsense." The church has no religious purpose other than to proclaim a gospel of grace that enables people to repent and turn to Christ for their salvation.

Thank God for His grace, which allows us to put our faith in Christ for salvation and live victorious lives.

Faith follows grace

Just as Abraham was declared righteous by his faith, so are we. *"The righteousness of God is revealed from faith to faith; as it is written, "The just shall live by faith" Romans 1:17.*

Faith is now something we exercise just like Abraham did. *"By faith, Abraham obeyed when he was called to go out to a place which he would receive as an inheritance went out not knowing where he was going. By faith he dwelt in the land of promise".*

It is no good saying, but I do not have faith. The Bible

says we all have a measure of faith. *"God has dealt to each one a measure of faith" Romans 12:3.*

That measure seems to vary according to our calling, gifting, ministry, and purpose in life. We should not overestimate or underestimate that measure of faith. The implication is that we should be operating within that measure of faith.

Day 13 (Journal)

I am feeling a bit down today, but by faith, I will overcome and continue my pursuit of God.

We have Barry Silverback taking lectures today. Barry is the founding pioneering father of the Christian Revival Crusade in PNG. I have known of Barry for some time as I was born again through the CRC in Australia. He has established a great church in Port Moresby with beautiful facilities.

Barry is well known and respected throughout the nation, and it is a pleasure to have him share this morning. Barry will be sharing on Principles of Leadership.

Lord, increase our faith

For my study, I am continuing today on the theme of faith. I thought of the disciples who came to Jesus and said, *"Lord, increase our faith." Luke 17:5.* I think we all want Jesus to increase our faith.

Jesus implies that if their faith was the size of a mustard seed, they could do great things. It seems it is not the quantity of faith we have but how we use it.

The right environment seems to give our faith a boost. Since I have been ministering in PNG, I have found that people are so receptive and responsive that my faith has increased. The right atmosphere releases faith.

The biggest hindrance to faith is unbelief. Even Jesus was restricted when people displayed unbelief. *"He could do no mighty works there, except that He laid His hands on a few sick people and healed them. And He marveled because of their unbelief."* Mark 6:5-6.

Once again, the environment or atmosphere seems to make a difference to our level of faith. Unbelief limits our faith and what we can accomplish in the name of the Lord.

Day 14 (Journal)

It is Saturday, and I am feeling much better today. I spent the day with the family. We drove up to Variata National Park and had a picnic with some other families from the church.

Maria Von Trapp was with us and played her accordion while we all sang along. Yes, Maria is from the original Von Trapp family from the movie 'Sound of Music.' Maria came to PNG as a missionary with the catholic church, but she mainly fellowships with us. She is a very gracious and lovely lady who has impacted the nation.

Chapter 12

Activate your faith

Day 15 (Journal)

Sunday morning again. Pastor Edward Oki led us in a beautiful time of worship.

We enjoyed having the late Pastor Trevor Chandler speak this morning. He was the pastor of a great church in Brisbane, Australia.

Trevor was a dynamic speaker, and the people loved him. He always starts with a joke, and this morning, he said, *"Did you hear that pastor Terry had a fire in his library? He was distraught because the fire burnt his only two colouring books."*

While Trevor was speaking, a fly kept buzzing around his head. He tried to brush it away, but it kept coming back. He opened his mouth at the wrong moment and swallowed the fly. He gulped and said, *"His mother will be pleased now that he is in the ministry."* Some people in the front row fell onto the floor laughing. He went on to preach a great word.

We were very thankful to Trevor and his church for picking up our support. The church we were from in Melbourne agreed to support us for twelve months. We were to return but decided to stay longer, so they dropped our support. We were devastated by their decision and thought we might have to return to Australia.

However, when Trevor, who was already partially supporting John Pasterkamp, found out, he told us not to worry that they would pick up our support for however long we wanted to stay.

We had to work on our attitude, but time heals, and we managed to maintain a good relationship with the church in Melbourne. However, when we eventually returned to Australia, we became a part of the network of churches under Trevor Chandler.

We spent a wonderful Sunday afternoon with several of our church leaders, Trevor, and the small team that came with him from Brisbane.

Day 16 (Journal)

Trevor Chandler and the team took lectures this morning. Trevor and a few from the team gave their testimonies. It was a powerful time.

Creating an atmosphere for faith

Inspired by Trevor, I decided to explore ways to create an atmosphere to strengthen our faith and give us more confidence when ministering. I ended up with four possible ways we can create an atmosphere that will help support our faith -

1. **Give people Hope** - Faith is the substance of things hoped for in *Hebrews 11:1*. Always be hopeful. Never take away a person's hope. Hope is the precursor to faith.

2. **Preach the Word of God** - Faith Comes by hearing the word of God *Romans 10:17*. We need to saturate ourselves and others in the word of God to see an increase in faith.

3. **Demonstrate love** - Faith grows and works in the atmosphere of love. We should love and care for others. *2 Thessalonians 1:3, Galatians 5:6.*

4. **Scatter seeds of faith** - Faith is like a seed; it needs to be sown continually into other people in seed form for us to reap a harvest. *Matthew 17:20*

Day 17 (Journal)

Pastor Trevor and the team continued to take lectures. After lectures, we piled into our Dyna Bus and gave Trevor and the team a tour around Port Moresby.

I managed to get some study in later in the day and continued on the theme of faith.

Act upon your faith

"Faith by itself, if it does not have works, it is dead; I will show you my faith by my works." James 2:17-18.

In this context, 'works' can be translated as actions. Smith Wigglesworth used to say the Acts of the Apostles were called 'Acts' because the Apostles acted. If we say we have faith, it should be evident to all as we act on it. Then, people will see our faith.

Jesus set the example, followed by the Apostles, by commending people for acting on their faith.

Here are just a few examples –

As YOU have believed so let it be to you. – Matt 8:13

When Jesus saw THEIR faith. – Matt 9:2

YOUR faith has made YOU well. – Matt 9:22

According to YOUR faith, let it be. – Matt 9:29

Great is YOUR faith; let it be to YOU. – Matt 15:28

Through faith in HIS Name. – Acts 3:16

Seeing HE had Faith to be healed. – Acts 14:9

Our faith is rewarded

The Bible promises that faith will be rewarded when we seek Him diligently.

"But without faith, it is impossible to please Him, for he who comes to God must believe that He is and that He is a rewarder of those who diligently seek Him." Hebrews 11:6.

We see that faith pleases God and that when we seek Him in faith, whether for wisdom, direction, guidance, healing, or just fellowship. He promises to reward us. That reward may be different from what we expect. For example, we may be seeking Him for healing, but the healing comes through us being led to the right specialist to treat and fix the problem.

You will find out how I felt God rewarded me after reading the last chapter.

Hungry For God

Chapter 13

What God wants in every Church

Day 18 (Journal)

I was feeling a little weak today. So I asked Pinaria Sialis, our current College Dean, to take lectures this morning.

Pinaria and his wife, Eloi, are ex-students with tremendous potential, and it is a blessing to have them run the daily routine of the College.

(Years later, Pinaria became the pastor of a great church in Lae and eventually the chairman of Christian Life Centre Churches in PNG).

After a good rest and a time of prayer, I went to study the word and looked at *1 Corinthians 13:13*. *"Now abides faith, hope, love, these three; but the greatest of these is love."*

I have been examining faith, and now I will look at what God expects to find in every church: faith, hope, and love. We see this strategically placed in the context of the gifts of the Holy Spirit and their operation.

We have already covered faith in previous chapters. So, let's look at the other two mentioned - hope and love.

Hope

We should never take hope away from someone; it might be all they have. We need to remember that hope is far better than being hopeless. Hope is like a Kickstarter for faith.

We should never give up on hope; while there is life, there is always hope. We have these beautiful verses to encourage us.

> *"For there is hope for a tree. If it is cut down, that it will sprout again, and that its tender shoots will not cease. Though its roots may grow old in the earth, and its stump may die in the ground. Yet at the scent of water, it will bud and bring forth branches like a plant". Job 14:7-9.*

The stump that is left may only need the scent of water to begin to sprout again. There is always hope for new life and new beginnings when you tap into the water of life, Christ Jesus our Lord.

However, those outside of Christ are like those with no hope. When they lose a loved one, the bible says they sorrow (or grieve) as someone with no hope. Their vision is confined to this earth, whereas Christians have an eternal hope centred on heaven.

"But I do not want you to be ignorant, brethren, concerning those who have fallen asleep, lest you sorrow as others who have no hope" 1 *Thessalonians 4:13*. Christians do not sorrow like those who have no hope, for they know they will be reunited one day with their loved ones in Heaven.

Hope leads us to faith. We read, *"Now faith is the substance of things hoped for the evidence of things not seen." Hebrews 11:1* When we hope for something, it is like a launching pad for faith.

No wonder the Apostle Paul said, *"Now may the God of Hope fill you with all joy in believing, that you may abound in hope by the power of the Holy Spirit."*

Hang on to hope. It brings about an atmosphere of faith, and your faith and patience enable you to obtain God's promises.

Day 19 (Journal)

I am feeling much better today, returning to my usual routine before heading for the hills to resume my time with the Lord. Pinaria is continuing with lectures to the students today.

Love

I have covered faith and hope; now, I will look at love as the greatest of the three. Why is love the greatest? In the context of 1 Corinthians 13, it is because -

"Love never fails" Verse 8.

Human love may fail, but not the love of God. Faith may fail, gifts of the Holy Spirit may fail, speaking in tongues and prophecy may fail, and our ability to feed the poor may fail. But we are told here in this context that the love of God will never fail.

Having all these wonderful gifts operating in a church means nothing if we do not have love. For God is love. I have heard preachers even speak on love. But off the platform, they seem to have no time or concern for anyone except their ministry.

We were at a conference recently and having lunch at a table next to one of the guest speakers, who had just brought a message on love and our need to accept everyone in a very passionate preaching style. However, this person had no time for us; they ignored us at the table, and it was as if we did not exist. We were very disappointed as far as we were concerned their message lost all credibility. We need to be careful to practice what we preach.

Jesus said, *"A new commandment I give unto you, that you love one another; as I have loved you, that you also love one another. By this the world will know you are my disciples". John 13:34-35.*

If the church is going to have an impact on the world,

we will need to be loving one another. The world will not be impressed if we lack unity and love; all they see is disunity, religiosity, liturgical ceremonies, or even the gifts of the Spirit. Still, if we do not love one another, we will lose our credibility.

Love is the greatest asset for any church.

Chapter 14
Equipped for Ministry

Day 20 (Journal)

I was feeling great today. I spent the morning in Bible College lecturing on principles of leadership.

I did some studying from home today.

I need an answer to a question on my mind. "Are we being adequately equipped for ministry?" I'm not just thinking of those who are in full-time ministry, but all believers. To what extent is every believer equipped for ministry?

Ascension Gift Ministries

The ascension gift ministries hold the key. *"When He ascended on high, He led captivity captive, and gave gifts to men"*...... *"And He Himself gave some to be apostles, some prophets, some evangelists, and some pastors and teachers for the equipping of the saints for the work of the ministry, for the edifying of the body of Christ" Ephesians 4:8-12.*

Let's pause and analise this section. There are five specialised ministry gifts that the Lord has given for the equipping of the saints for the work of the ministry. (Apostles, Prophets, Evangelists, Pastors, and Teachers).

Believers should sit under all of these gifts at some stage. It may be hard for some smaller churches where the pastor feels he has to be all five of these gifts. The pastor should endeavour to put himself, his leaders, and the congregation under these gifts by inviting them to his church or encouraging his people to go to conferences or watch videos rather than trying to be all of these gifts.

When I first got saved in a little church in my country town, the minister saw potential in me and took me to several large conferences where these five ministry gifts were operating. It was a real eye-opener, and it helped me grow spiritually and have a vision for ministry and the Body of Christ.

These five ministry gifts have the task of 'equipping' the saints (believers) for the work of the ministry. 'Equipping' can be likened to an adequately equipped rescue unit, like fully trained and equipped paramedics. When I retired, I did some rescue work with Volunteer Marine Rescue.

We were responsible for helping people in trouble on the water. We trained in first aid, boat skills, and maintenance. The boats had to be equipped so we were ready to deal with all kinds of medical emergencies, breakdowns, and vessels that ran aground or had mechanical problems. The church should be like a rescue unit fully equipped to minister and preach the gospel, save people, and bring them to maturity in Christ.

Training

Training does not happen automatically.

We must labour to train and equip believers to do the work of the ministry. It is primarily to help us maintain the unity of the faith, increase our knowledge of Christ, and bring us to a place of ministry where we can serve one another until we reach maturity in Christ.

> *"For the edifying of the body of Christ, till we all come to the unity of the faith and of the knowledge of the Son of God, to a perfect man, to the measure of the stature of the fullness of Christ." Ephesians 4:12-13.*

Maturity brings stability so that every wind of doctrine does not infiltrate the church. It will help us to avoid being deceived and divided.

> *"That we should no longer be children tossed to and fro and carried about with every wind of doctrine, by the trickery of men, in the cunning craftiness of deceitful plotting." Ephesians 4:14.*

Everybody needs to contribute

It goes on to admonish us to minister the truth in love, where Christ is the head of the church, and that we all have a part to play by contributing to the body of Christ. Whatever gifting we may have, the body edifies itself in love. *"...By which every part does its share, causes growth of the body for the edifying of itself in love." Ephesians 4:15-16.*

Apart from exposure to the fivefold ministry gifts. If

believers and churches are to mature, here are some practical keys that will help local pastors equip the saints –

1. **Prayer** – The old saying is, "Those who pray together stay together."

2. **The word of God** – Needs to be preached, taught, and put into practice.

3. **Discipleship Training** – On-the-job practical training for all believers.

4. **Spiritual Gifts** – Sensitivity to operate freely in the gifts of the Holy Spirit.

5. **Mixing with others** – Being connected to other members of the body of Christ and the local community.

The church is becoming mature, and by doing these things, it will grow in unity, love, and grace, which will positively affect its community.

Day 21 (Journal)

Saturday, taking the day off to spend time with the family. We went to Ella Beach for a swim. The water was so warm, almost like a bath. We had a lovely time together.

Chapter 15
The Dealings of God

Day 22 (Journal)

I have just broken another personal milestone, having accomplished a 21-day fast, like in the book of Daniel.

Today is Sunday. Edward Oki led the worship this morning, and it was a fantastic time in the presence of the Lord. Edward and his wife Anne are ex-students and a wonderful couple.

We are honored to have Peter Clyburn and Pamela Beaumont speaking this morning.

Peter is from Australia, and Pamela is from New Zealand. They run "Freedom Bible School" in the heart of the jungle in Bougainville. They both have excellent teaching skills, speak fluently in Pidgin English, and communicate well with the students.

Rewind for a moment - I will never forget my first trip

to Bougainville. I was on a ministry trip from Melbourne (before God called me to PNG). I flew from Port Moresby to Kieta. Then we went to Sue and Don Ware's house. Don was working at the Bougainville Copper Mine. Years later, the mine had to close down because Bougainville wanted to become independent from PNG and formed the BRA (Bougainville Revolutionary Army). The mine ended up in a war zone fighting against PNG troops. The war lasted many years before the BRA surrendered and decided to remain as part of PNG.

Sue said she would take me to the Bible School with Judi Jones (nee Paddock), who was doing mission work in PNG. They looked at me in my polished shoes, pressed trousers, and shirt and said, "Do you have any old shoes and clothes." I said, "No, Why?" They said, "It is a long trip on rough roads, and if it has been raining in the mountains, the roads will be muddy and slippery." Well, they sure got that right!

We piled into a little 4-wheel drive Suzuki, and off we went. The road was great up until we reached the mine. After we drove through the mine area, the road was terrible. Some of the potholes in the road seemed as big as the Suzuki; it had been raining, we got bogged a few times, and I had to help push the Suzuki out, so much for my polished shoes and good trousers. We also had to drive through rivers that were quite deep. It was all happening in the steamy heat amid the dense jungle. I could not help admiring these brave women willing to drive me through this terrain.

We finally arrived at the Bible School and met Peter and

Pamela. I was impressed with the way they were running the school. Seeing this well-organised school in the middle of the jungle was astonishing, with so many students taught the word of God.

We eventually arrived back that night. I believe that trip seeded thoughts in my mind for the Bible College we would later establish in Port Moresby.

Fast forward - We did not realise at the time that some years later, Don and Sue and their girls, Tanya, Kate, and Debbie, would be in the church we were to lead in Lismore, Australia. They were a lovely, hospitable family who ministered to many who needed encouragement and help.

While living in PNG, I had many adventurous trips back to Bougainville to meet with Pastor Barry Winton, who came from Australia to pastor the church in Arawa. Barry and I drove down to Siwai several times in a little 4-wheel drive Suzuki to speak at special camp meetings. We saw many saved, baptised, healed, and set free due to these camp meetings.

During one of these camp meetings, I will never forget some people who had radios (there was no TV) who came to us and said things like, "It is the end of the world." The radio reception was poor. Something was happening, but we had no idea what was going on. A week later, when we got back to civilisation, we discovered that it was all about the tragedy of the 9/11 attack on the United States of America.

Pastor Uzziah Movo led the church after Barry and Joan left. Uzziah was a Bible College graduate and became involved in peace negotiations after the BRA submitted again to PNG rule. Pastor David Damette, another graduate, led the churches in the Siawai area for some time after the war.

Fast forward - Barry and Joan left Bougainville a year after we left PNG. We had started an outreach from Lismore at Kyogle and invited Barry and Joan to come and establish it as a church. They came and ended up pioneering a great church in Kyogle; they secured an excellent facility for the church.

Many people refer to Bougainville as 'Beautiful Bougainville,' and it is, with its dense jungle, lovely beaches, big rivers, and rugged mountains with at least one smoldering volcano.

Back to Sunday - They spoke about the dealings of God. We spent the rest of the day entertaining Peter and Pamela. A few years later, Peter married Marion, and they both ran the Bible school in Bougainville together with Pamela before returning to Australia. Pamela eventually returned to New Zealand.

Day 23 (Journal)

This morning, we broke the students into two groups. Peter spoke to the men. Pamela spoke to the women. They were dealing with some cultural issues and how to communicate the gospel.

After Peter and Pamela spoke on the dealings of God, I thought I would do some more study and dig a little deeper into this subject.

No one is exempt

It would appear from scripture that no one is exempt from the dealings of God. When God deals with us, it is usually through some trials that test our faith, but at the same time, He strengthens our character. We can have all the Charisma in the world, but sometimes, God has to refine our character.

If we step out of line or are in danger of making a fool of ourselves or doing something stupid, God may need to discipline us as a loving father would his son or daughter.

As a Father disciplines his son

When a father disciplines his son, he wants to correct him and help him avoid serious trouble.

As a father, I wouldn't say I liked disciplining my children and would sometimes sidestep the issue or hand it over to my wife. But I knew in my heart that it was the right thing to do for their sake. The problem is our children sometimes do not understand why we must discipline them at the time.

There are many different ways we can apply discipline. When I was a boy at school, it was a leather strap. You were required to put out your hand if you were naughty while the teacher whacked it with the belt, sometimes several times. It was a bit the same for me at home, but I usually got the strap around the legs. Even though the bible says, *"Do not spare the rod,"* that standard of discipline is no longer acceptable in our society because of past abuses. Today, discipline is usually applied by taking away privileges, like using a mobile phone or computer.

God disciplines out of love

We need to know that when God disciplines us, it is out of love. It is for our good.

> *"My son, do not despise the chastening of the Lord, nor be discouraged when you are rebuked of Him; for whom the Lord loves, He chastens." Hebrews 12:5-6.*

God loves us so much that he must sometimes chasten, discipline, and correct us in love. It is for our benefit, not His.

> *"But if you are without chastening, of which all have become partakers, then you are illegitimate and not sons" Hebrews 12:8.*

The implication is that if God were not to discipline us, He would be irresponsible and not treat us as true sons.

Painful but profitable

We do not like to be chastised by anyone, let alone God. We can become sad and discouraged and feel it is just not fair. It may be painful but profitable for us.

> *"…..He for our profit that we may partake of His holiness. Now no chastening seems to be joyful for the present, but painful; yet afterward it yields the peaceable fruit of righteousness to those who have been trained by it". Hebrews 12:10-11.*

Discipline is not a time of joy; it can be painful sometimes, but those who accept it are trained by it. It yields the peaceable fruit of righteousness, which is profitable for us and others we fellowship with, whether family or church members.

Chapter 16

Waiting upon the Lord

Day 24 (Journal)

I had a good time taking lectures this morning on 'The Promise of the Father,' which was about how God promised to send the Holy Spirit.

I drove up into the hills again. While praising God and praying, I noticed this majestic eagle circling effortlessly in the heavens. As I was watching, I thought of the scripture in Isaiah.

> *"Those who wait on the Lord shall renew their strength; they shall mount up like eagles, they shall run and not be weary, they shall walk and not faint" Isaiah 40:31.*

It is an inspiring scripture for people who have become weary, weak, and in danger of giving up.

Finding time to wait

It is not easy to find time to wait. We have learned to be in a hurry to survive our busy modern-day lifestyle.

Waiting upon the Lord renews our strength, and just like the eagle I was watching, we soar above the problems that make us weary. We begin to see things from a different perspective. As a result, we can find the energy and strength to refocus and pursue our calling to God.

What does it mean to wait on the Lord? It means what I am doing now by studying, praying, fasting, worshipping, and spending time in His presence.

We live in a world where this would seem like a waste of time for the natural mind. We are always in a hurry to do something. We live in a world of instant everything, and besides coffee, we have mobile phones, computers, microwaves, freeways, supermarkets, and takeaway foods. We are constantly in a hurry and always on the move.

We do not like waiting for anything. I was in line at a church recently, waiting my turn to help myself to coffee after the service, and I had this woman behind me say, "Come on, hurry up; we haven't got all day." I was going as fast as I could for my age. Yes, you do not expect that kind of attitude at church.

We are impatient even in our relationship with God. Our Western style of praying is a bit like that old saying, "Lord, give me patience, and give it to me now."

Day 25 (Journal)

I took lectures this morning, still on the theme of 'The Promise of the Father.' After classes, I stayed home today to study 'Waiting on God.'

A spiritual discipline

Waiting upon the Lord is a spiritual discipline. It does not come automatically in this world where we are constantly under pressure to be doing something. We feel we have to be in charge and that we need to take control of a situation as quickly as possible.

Some dictionary definitions for 'Waiting' are 'Deferring action or departure until something expected occurs.' 'Waiting until it is your turn to do something.' 'To remain in a state where you expect or hope something will happen soon.'

If we could only learn to wait upon the Lord, we would renew our strength spiritually and mentally and be more effective in ministry.

"Therefore I will look to the Lord; I will wait for the God of my salvation; my God will hear me." Micah 7:7. May we wait patiently in faith, expecting Him to hear and respond to us.

The purpose of waiting

The primary purpose of waiting upon the Lord is to renew our strength, soar above our problems like the eagle I have been watching, and begin seeing things differently.

When God answers us, we have renewed confidence in His will. Answers to prayer give us inner peace, and there is no better feeling than to know God has heard you.

There are several things we are allowing God to do in our lives as we wait upon Him –

1. Strengthen our faith

2. Test and purify our motives

3. Increase our thanks and praise

4. Re-arrange our priorities

5. Take control of our destiny

Power from on high

Another significant result of waiting on the Lord is to be endured with power from high.

> *"Behold I send the promise of the Father upon you, but tarry in the city of Jerusalem until you are endued with power from on high." Luke 24:49.*

Jesus had also said to His disciples, *"You shall receive power when the Holy Spirit has come upon you; and you shall be witnesses to Me in Jerusalem, and in all Judea and Samaria, and to the end of the earth." Acts 1:8.*

The first outpouring of this power was poured upon the waiting disciples as they prayed in the upper room on the day of Pentecost. We call this the baptism in the Holy Spirit. The evidence of this happening throughout the New Testament was people speaking in other tongues.

Speaking in other tongues

'And they were all filled with the Holy Spirit and began to speak in other tongues, as the Spirit gave them the utterance.' Acts 2:4.

After the day of Pentecost, there were several times when believers were baptised in the Holy Spirit and spoke in other tongues.

"The gift of the Holy Spirit had been poured out on the Gentiles also, for they heard them speak with other tongues and glorify God." Acts 10:45-46.

Is there some advantage for believers who can speak in other tongues? Paul makes it clear that it is very beneficial for believers in *1 Corinthians 14:1-4* he states –

1. We speak directly to God

2. We speak mysteries in the Spirit

3. We edify ourselves

There are other scriptures to support this and those that speak about praying in the spirit, including speaking in other tongues.

During this time of fasting and prayer, I have been spending much time speaking in other tongues, which has been a source of strength.

You, too, can be endured with supernatural power from on high by being baptised in the power of the Holy Spirit.

Chapter 17

The cross, the serpent, the Son

Day 26 (Journal)

I took lectures this morning.

After lectures, I was doing some work outside our security fence. David and Clara Muap lived next door. Their son Johnathan was watching me with his pet puppy when, out of the corner of my eye, I saw a Papuan Black Snake, which is poisonous and deadly, heading straight toward Johnathan. Before I could react, the puppy jumped between the snake and Johnathan. The snake bit the puppy, turned away, and quickly disappeared into some long grass nearby.

I yelled out to David and told him what had just happened. He came and rushed the puppy off to a vet, but it was dead by the time he arrived.

After this, I was in shock and decided to stay home to

meditate on the cross concerning what I had just witnessed. I began to think about the serpent's bite.

We have all been bitten because of sin and face the death penalty. But, the Son of God, Jesus, like the puppy, stepped in to save us by dying on the cross. We, like Johnathan, were saved because of Jesus, who thankfully rose from the dead as our Saviour and Lord.

I will follow this theme tomorrow.

Day 27 (Journal)

Pinaria Sialis took lectures today. I rested in the morning and then headed to study and pray for my spot in the hills.

Continuing to meditate on the cross because of what happened yesterday. The scripture that came to mind was where Jesus said,

The cross of Calvary

> *"As Moses lifted up the serpent in the wilderness, even so, must the Son of Man be lifted up, that whoever believes in Him should not perish but have eternal life." John 3:14-15.*

Jesus is pointing to being lifted up on the cross, but why has He mentioned Moses lifting up the serpent in the wilderness? What is the point of Him referring to this story?

The people had become discouraged in the wilderness and started to murmur against God and Moses.

The serpents bite

"So the Lord sent fiery serpents among the people, and they bit the people, and many of the people of Israel died." Numbers 21:6.

The people realised they had sinned and asked Moses to pray that the Lord would remove the serpents. So Moses prayed for the people.

When Moses prayed, the Lord answered Moses and said to him, *"Make a fiery serpent, and set it on a pole; and it shall be that everyone who is bitten when he looks at it shall live. So Moses made a bronze serpent, and put it on a pole; and so it was if a serpent had bitten anyone when he looked at the bronze serpent, he lived". Numbers 21:8-9.*

Today, The serpent's bite represents the penalty for our sins: death. We are all victims of the serpent's bite because of our sins. We return to the Garden of Eden, where the serpent (Satan) bit Adam and Eve by deceiving them to disobey God and fall into sin.

The Son of God, our Saviour

The bronze serpent on a pole is like Christ on the cross, symbolizing Divine Judgement. The Altar in the Tabernacle was overlaid with bronze, and it was where the animals were sacrificed to atone for the sins of the people. God Judged sin when Jesus died on the cross so that we would escape judgment for our sins.

Today, all we have to do is look upon Christ and believe, and we will be delivered from the serpent's bite and the gates of hell and know we have eternal life in heaven.

Therefore, we can take comfort in this scripture *"For the wages of sin is death, but the gift of God is eternal life in Christ Jesus our Lord." Romans 6:23.*

It is all good news

What appeared to be bad news when Jesus was crucified is good news for us. Without his sacrificial death and shed blood, there would be no forgiveness of sin. The word 'gospel' means good news; it is the best news anyone can ever receive.

"For I am not ashamed of the gospel of Christ, for it is the power of God to salvation to everyone who believes" Romans 1:16.

Paul is writing to the church in Rome, which was probably intimidated by the mighty Roman empire that ruled the world at the time. He is saying there is nothing to be ashamed of or intimidated by. Rome, with all its power, is still inferior to the power of the gospel that can bring salvation.

We should never be ashamed of the message of the cross; this is good news and the only power to save us from our sins and give us eternal life.

Chapter 18
A Zeal for the house of God

Day 28 (Journal)

Being a Saturday, I spent a relaxed day with the family. We drove to downtown Port Moresby, then back past Hanabadu Village around the bay and back to our home in Waigani.

You could still see the wreck of the MV MacDui in the harbour that was sunk by Japanese bombers during the second world war. Due to the war, many wrecked planes, tanks, and guns were scattered throughout PNG.

My Dad visited us from Australia, and because his twin brother and many he knew fought on the Kokoda trail, I took him to the Bomana War Memorial Cemetary. As we walked around the graves, I was amazed at how young some were, around 18 to 25. Now and then, he would stop and wipe tears from his eyes when he recognised the name of a mate he grew up with as a boy. It was the only time I remember my dad weeping.

While my dad was with us, I took him on a flight that landed at several airports, including the village of Kokoda. It was called 'The Milk Run,' It was a reasonably small plane that took a few passengers and some cargo. I could not believe the skill of the pilots flying between the rugged mountains and how they could land and take off on some of the most precarious runways on Earth. It was a scary ride, and we were glad to return to Port Moresby in one piece.

Day 29 (Journal)

It was Sunday, and Pastor David Muap led the service. It was a beautiful time of worship. David and his wife Clara are also ex-students. David is on the ministry team in Port Moresby.

Pastor Isaac Alipet, a former student now pastoring in the 'Duke of York Islands' is sharing this morning. He shared a great word on 'Revival in the Islands.'

Rewind for a moment - Isaac was already a pastor in the beautiful Duke of York Islands off the coast of Rabaul when he enrolled in Bible College. After he had graduated from our college last year, he had arranged to take me to his home Village in the Duke of York Islands.

We got on a crowded boat in the harbour at Rabaul (well before the volcano had erupted and destroyed the town). We left late in the day. It was dark when we arrived at the Duke of York Islands, and we had to drop people off at different islands. I could see flashes of white through the darkness as waves broke on the reefs. The boat's captain did a great job threading through the reefs until we arrived at Isaac's Island.

We went straight to his house in the village, and we both slept on some very thin mattresses on the floor. In the middle of the night, I heard strange noises above us. I shone my torch, and some giant rats ran around on the rafters. I woke Isaac and told him. He said, "They are always around; they won't bite you," then he rolled over and went back to sleep.

I woke up early the following day and decided to go for a walk. I was overwhelmed by the beauty of the place. The village stretched along the shoreline of a pristine white sandy beach; the water was crystal clear, and in the distance, you could see the silhouette of other nearby islands glistening in the early morning light. I thought, wow, what a paradise; I could live here.

Isaac had arranged for me to speak at a Uniting Church camp. People had gathered from the other islands. It was a great time; people came to Christ, and many were healed and delivered.

The Uniting Church Bishop came from Rabaul. He was sitting in the front row when demons began to manifest; people started throwing their beetle nut, cigarettes, and poison powder used by sorcerers out the open sides of the building and came to the front, repenting of their sins in front of the Bishop. I will never forget the amazement on his face as he stamped his feet up and down with what appeared to be a mixture of fear, awe, and excitement. At the end of the Camp, we had people line up on the shoreline to be baptised in the sea. The Bishop was in his element as he and other pastors baptised about 50 people.

Back to Sunday morning. After Isaac spoke, we spent some time fellowshipping with him and several other families in the Bible College.

Day 30 (Journal)

After taking lectures and doing my usual routine, I headed for the hills to pray and study.

Are you zealous?

I felt the Lord was challenging me to be zealous for Him and the Church, not just the local church, but the whole Body of Christ.

In Revelation, we read how the Lord rebuked the church at Laodicea for being lukewarm. *"I know your works that you are neither cold nor hot. I could wish you were cold or hot. So then because you are lukewarm and neither cold nor hot, I will vomit you out of my mouth". Revelation 3:15-16.*

The question is, why or how did the church become lukewarm? Reading the context, it seems the Laodicean church was wealthy. They thought they needed nothing and were blind to their spiritual poverty. It sounds very much like some churches I know today.

The Lord is not impressed with lukewarmness. What should we do about it? The answer is in *Verse 19. "As many as I love, I rebuke and chasten. Therefore, be ZEALOUS and repent".*

Out of love, God will rebuke and discipline us. How should we respond? We must repent and become zealous, enthusiastic, eager, and willing to get back on track spiritually. The Lord wants us to be hot and on fire for Him.

A misguided zeal

Some Christians and Churches have a zeal but not according to the zeal God is looking for in His people.

> *"For I bear them witness that they have a zeal for God, but not according to knowledge. For they being ignorant of God's righteousness, and seeking to establish their own righteousness, have not submitted to the righteousness of God". Romans 10:2-3.*

We can be ignorant of Godly zeal by following rules that we think are right and trying to establish our righteousness. But our futile works do not impress God; they do not align with His righteousness.

Have you ever attended a lukewarm church? I have been to churches where everything is routine and dry, in the sense that the service is all mapped out with a liturgy and a repetitive ceremony every year. They were oblivious to their spiritual poverty. There was no room for the spontaneity of the Holy Spirit. I know the people appear sincere but ignorant of what God expects. How did I feel? Just like Jesus did about the Lukewarm church at Laodicea.

Jesus was zealous

Jesus shocked everybody, including His disciples, when He became angry and made a whip and drove out those doing business in the temple, telling them that His Father's House was to be a House of prayer and not a house of merchandise.

"When He had made a whip of cords, He drove them all out of the temple, with sheep and the oxen, and poured out the changer's money and overturned the tables. And He said to those who sold doves, Take these things away! Do not make My Father's House a house of merchandise. Then His disciples remembered it was written, *"ZEAL for your house has eaten me up." John 2:15-17.*

When His disciples saw Him like this, they remembered where it was written, *'Zeal for my Father's house has eaten me up.' (Psalm 69:9).*

What does it mean to be eaten up with zeal? It means that you are consumed with a passion for something. You are like a dog with a bone and will not let it go until you accomplish your objectives.

When I start writing, I am so zealous it consumes my time and energy until I finish.

Everyone would have expected the Messiah to attack the Gentiles for their beliefs and practices. But here He is laying into the Jews and rebuking them for their ways. But it shows us how zealous the Lord is for His house and how zealous we should be for the church today.

It is up to us!

We need to repent of our lukewarmness and become more zealous for God. But it begins with us.

Paul told Timothy to stir up the gift of God within him. *"I remind you to stir up the gift of God which is in you through the laying on of my hands." 2 Timothy 1:6.*

I'm not suggesting that Timothy was lukewarm. I'm trying to make a point that we are responsible for stirring ourselves up to become more zealous and proactive in whatever God has called us to do in the life of His church.

Chapter 19

Do not fear the future

Day 31 (Journal)

I'm feeling good and thinking I can make it to 40 days now. We have Arthur Blessitt sharing with the students today. Arthur has carried a cross around the world and throughout PNG.

I walked around parts of Port Moresby with Arthur carrying his cross a little over a month ago. When a large crowd gathered, he would stand his cross up, preach, and give an altar call for salvation. Hundreds responded, probably thousands throughout the nation. His impact has been so significant that after his lecture to the students this morning, he has a meeting with the Prime Minister.

I sat in on Arthur's message to the students, and it was a brilliant message on 'Spiritual development in leadership.'

He based his message on *Luke 21:25-26*. *"And on Earth distress of nations….Men's hearts failing them from fear and the expectation of those things coming on the earth".*

Arthur expounded this scripture on how we will all be affected by fear in these last days. He challenged the students by saying, "Fear can make your study worthless; you may have all the answers, you may have a thorough knowledge of the Bible, you may have excelled in theology, you may be thoroughly trained to minister, but if you are afraid God will not be able to use you, as Christians we need to be free of fear." He went on to say a lot more, most of which I transcribed in my book, 'Unlocking Your Purpose.'

He said one simple thing that has stayed with me all these years: "It's not the clothes you wear; it's the way you wear them." He was referring to our demeanor. The way you hold yourself and the way you walk. You are a son and daughter of God.

'Fear nots' in the Bible

After listening to Arthur, I headed for my study and started studying the 'Fear Nots' in the bible. I heard someone say there are 365 in the Bible, one for each day. It sounds so good; I have never bothered to count them.

Fast forward a moment. I was traveling to Myanmar (Burma) together with Denis Barnard. Our mission was to smuggle Bibles hidden in our luggage to a contact we had from the 'Brother Andrew' organisation in Rangoon. Myanmar was under strict Military rule at the time, and there was no absolute freedom for the churches, and some Christians were persecuted for their faith.

The night before we flew in, I had a nightmare. We were apprehended for smuggling bibles and lined up against a wall to be shot. When I woke up, I prayed and asked the Lord for reassurance that we would be okay. He gave me this scripture

"Fear not, for I am with you; be not dismayed, for I am your God. I will strengthen you; yes I will help you; I will uphold you with my right hand." Isaiah 41:10.

I needed that word. As the plane landed, it was announced that all luggage would be X-rayed. We were heading for the X-ray machine when an official stepped in front of us and pointed us away from the X-ray machine and customs toward the exit. Yes, thank you, Lord, for that word. He stepped in and helped us just like in the above scripture.

A spirit of fear (Journal)

There is a healthy fear that stops us from doing stupid things like defying the law of gravity and jumping off a high cliff.

But there is also a spirit of fear that intimidates us. It stops us from stepping out in faith and being the person God wants us to be. It is not from God.

"For God has NOT given us a spirit of fear, but of power and of love and a sound mind." 2 Timothy 1:7.

It would seem from the context that young Timothy may have been fearful at times and intimidated by people and the demands of the ministry. Paul needed to remind him that God had not given him a spirit of fear and encouraged him to stir up the gift of God within him and step out in faith as a man of God.

Fear not, little Flock

As I read the bible, this verse jumped out at me, *"Do not fear little flock, for it is your Father's good pleasure to give you the kingdom." Luke 12:32.*

I started to think about all the little churches in cities, towns, or villages and how insignificant they may feel compared to multitudes of unreached people who need to hear the gospel. I know some pastors and churches that feel that way.

Jesus uses the term 'little flock' to refer to His sheep (in churches) compared to our world system. We are well and truly outnumbered. He tells us that we, as Christians, have been sent into the world like sheep among wolves. *"I send you out as sheep in the midst of wolves." Matthew 10:16.*

However, we are not to be afraid. Jesus said, *"Fear not, little flock."* Why does He say that? Because he is our shepherd. No matter how overwhelmed we may feel by the world and the task of spreading the gospel, He will shepherd, lead, and guide us.

The keys to the kingdom

The rest of the verse assures us that it is the Father's pleasure to give us the kingdom. In His infinite wisdom, God has given His 'little flock' the keys to the kingdom of God.

No matter how insignificant you may feel, God has

entrusted you with the kingdom's keys. You hold what the world desperately needs: the gospel of the kingdom. The good news is that people can be saved and find eternal life through faith in Christ and a willingness to repent. Wow, how significant is that?

Jesus said to Peter, *"I will give you the keys to the kingdom of heaven." Matthew 16:19.* This was not exclusively for Peter, but for the Church.

At the moment on earth, the kingdom of God is not literal. It is the spiritual alternative to this world system. *'For the kingdom of God is not eating and drinking, but righteousness and peace and joy in the Holy Spirit." Romans 14:17.* (This is comforting when you are fasting).

If we are to enter the kingdom, Jesus said we must be born again, speaking of a spiritual birth that occurs when we believe in Jesus for our salvation.

Salvation begins with repentance, or a change of direction by turning away from sin and to God. It was at the heart of Jesus' preaching *'Repent, for the kingdom of heaven is at hand." Matthew 4:17*

Go into all the world

Jesus gave the great commission to take this message to the whole world. No matter how small or insignificant you or your church may feel, God trusts you to do your bit and proclaim the gospel. If we all, as believers, proclaim the gospel of the kingdom, it will be preached in all the world before Jesus returns.

Jesus said, *'This gospel of the kingdom will be preached in all the world as a witness to all nations, and then the end will come.'* Matthew 24:14.

Jesus said, *"Fear not, little flock,"* not to be intimidated by the world and the enormity of the task before us. What a tremendous privilege and responsibility we have to reach the world. It is all part of God's plan, even though it may be little by little, little flock. Remember, He is with us as we go.

Chapter 20

The message of the cross

Day 32 (Journal)

This morning, we have pastor Charles Lapa taking the students on evangelism. Charles has been walking with Arthur Blessitt throughout the country and has arranged much of his itinerary. Charles and his wife Lucy are ex-students and pastor a church and a halfway house for converted rascals in Morata (a nearby suburb).

In English, a rascal is often called a naughty or cheeky child. However, in PNG, rascal gangs are unruly armed criminals who steal, rape, and even murder people. Charles has an evangelistic gift and holds open-air rallies where gang leaders and members get saved. But they need to be rehabilitated in the halfway house. Charles operates under the banner of Life Ministry Outreach Centre, focusing on evangelism and reaching out to the lost.

Charles is from the Southern Highlands, and I remember traveling with him to his home village in a very rugged mountainous area of the Highlands. We had a great time.

Charles is well respected today by other pastors and leaders in the community for the tremendous impact he has had on the nation.

I am not an evangelist; my gifting is that of a pastor and teacher, but I have had to adapt in PNG to become more of an evangelist.

We all have a responsibility to be a witness for Christ, which is like being an evangelist. We may not have the gift of an evangelist, but as believers, we all need to do what we can to reach the lost.

Rewind for a moment - An American representative from the Billy Graham organisation came and shared with the students. As a result of having them minister, the organization invited me to attend a conference in Amsterdam for church leaders, pastors, and evangelists. It was a fantastic conference. Some 5,000 were in attendance.

In one of the sessions, Billy Graham said he preached a message early in his ministry that seemed to fall flat. He asked his team why he felt that way, and they said, "Because you didn't preach the cross." So ever since then, he has endeavoured to mention the cross in every message he preaches.

The message of the cross (Journal)

The apostle Paul knew how powerful the message of the cross was to him. *"For I determined not to know anything among you except Jesus Christ and him crucified." 1 Corinthians 2:2.*

The cross is at the heart of the gospel message. Jesus had to shed his blood, die, and rise from the dead before we could be saved. *"In whom we have redemption through His blood, the forgiveness of sins." Colossians 1:14.* We read in Hebrews without the shedding of blood, there is no forgiveness of sins. *(Hebrews 9:22)*

Why did Jesus stay on the cross?

When Jesus was nailed to the cross, people started to mock Him. *"Those who passed by blasphemed Him, wagging their heads and saying, "You who destroy the temple and build it in three days save Yourself! If you are the Son of God, come down from the cross". Likewise, the chief priests, also mocking with the scribes and elders, said, "He saved others; Himself He can not save. If He is the king of Israel, let Him now come down from the cross, and we will believe Him." Matthew 27:40-42.*

They were mocking Him, calling on Him to come down from the cross, and we will believe. They were looking for a supernatural manifestation of power to prove He was the Son of God. He could have made a great show and stepped down from the cross.

When Peter drew his sword and cut off the high priest's ear, Jesus rebuked him and said, *"Do you think that I cannot now pray to My Father, and He will provide Me with more than twelve legions of angels? How then could the scripture be fulfilled? it must happen this way." Matthew 26:53.*

So it would have been possible for Jesus to call on angels and miraculously step down from the cross for all to see. He could not do that. Why not? They would have then believed He was the son of God. The answer is in the last part of the above verse. How could the scriptures be fulfilled? It must happen this way.

He stayed there to become the sacrificial lamb for all humanity. He stayed there to secure our salvation.

Yes, He stayed there to shed His blood for you and me. Otherwise, we would have been lost in our sins for eternity. But now we can rejoice, for we have salvation and eternal life because Jesus stayed on the cross. **Thank God for the cross!**

Chapter 21

Walking with God

Day 33 (Journal)

Another bowel movement today. I have had nothing to eat; where is it coming from? I'm losing a lot of weight now, feeling good, but not much energy.

Pastor Leka Kemma is sharing with the students today. Leka is an ex-student now pastoring a Kerema church in the Gulf Province.

Rewind for a moment. Leka had invited me a little while ago to come and speak in his church. I had a great weekend of meetings, with the highlight being Sunday night. The Church met in a big open area under a house. The place was packed with people, and it was getting dark. He had asked me to speak on "Deliver us from evil," emphasizing the deliverance ministry.

When I started to pray for people, there were demonic

manifestations everywhere. It became very noisy, and being in a semi-residential area, some neighbours were very concerned.

It was not long before the police arrived in two four-wheel drive vehicles and parked out the front with lights flashing. They surrounded the house but did not come into the yard. They understood what was happening.

People came forward for salvation and healing. I had one man who came forward saying he had gone blind. He fell on the floor begging for forgiveness, and we prayed for his eyes to be opened again so he could see and receive Christ as his Saviour. I found out later that he was unsaved and came as a sorcerer to interrupt the meeting. But God had everything under control. What a miraculous way to get saved.

Back to lectures. Leka shared his testimony, how he was called into ministry, and his walk with God since then.

After lectures, I took Caroline shopping again and stayed home to study the theme of walking with God.

What does it mean to walk with God? How can we walk with God? Does it make a difference? I began to think of different ones that walked with God.

Adam and Eve

We go way back to the Garden of Eden. It is implied that they walked with God in the Garden.

> *"They heard the sound of the Lord walking in the garden in the cool of the day"* Genesis 3:8.

What an awesome picture that conjures up in the mind. Just imagine walking with God in the garden in the cool of the day and perhaps watching the sunset on the horizon.

What a privilege, but they messed it up by sinning against God. As a result, they were separated from God and banished from the garden. Only now, through Christ, is fellowship with God again restored so that humanity can walk with God.

Enoch walked with God

There are three primary references to Enoch walking with God; the first one is astonishing, *"So the days of Enoch were three hundred and sixty-five years (the number of days in a year). And Enoch walked with God; and he was not, for God took him." Genesis 5:23-24.* Enoch had a close relationship with God, so close that God took Him. Whoosh, Amazing!

We learn more about how Enoch walked with God in *Hebrews 11:5-6*. *"By faith, Enoch was taken away so he did not see death, and was not found because God had taken him; for before he was taken he had this testimony, that he pleased God. But without faith, it is impossible to please Him."*

Enoch pleased God so much he did not see death. He walked with God in faith. We cannot please God unless we also walk with Him in faith.

The last reference is in Jude, where he writes out of concern for what he sees happening in the church. *"For certain men have crept in unnoticed, who long ago were marked out for this condemnation, ungodly men, who turn the grace of our God into lewdness and deny the only Lord God of our Father Jesus Christ." Jude 4.* Jude continues to list all the evil influences creeping into the church and the impending judgment they face in the future.

Then Jude declares, *'Enoch the seventh from Adam, prophesied about these men also saying, "Behold the Lord comes with ten thousand of His saints to execute judgment on all, to convict all who are ungodly among them of all their ungodly deeds, which they have committed in an ungodly way, and of all the harsh things which ungodly sinners have spoken against Him." Jude 14-15.*

It would appear that Enoch pleased God by living by faith and not defiling himself with ungodly sinners. We still need to reach out to sinners with the gospel but not defile ourselves by becoming like them.

There seems to be a pattern emerging where walking with God is by faith in God and separation from an ungodly lifestyle.

Noah walked with God

In Genesis, we read that God was upset by the wickedness on the earth, but Noah found grace in the eyes of the Lord. Noah did what would have seemed a crazy thing to do in those days. By faith, he obeyed God and built an Ark according to God's blueprint because God was about to judge an evil world with a flood.

> *"Noah was a just man, perfect in his generation. Noah walked with God." Genesis 6:9.*

> *"By faith Noah, being divinely warned of things not yet seen, moved with godly fear, prepared an ark for the saving of his household, by which he condemned the world and became heir of the righteousness which is according to faith." Hebrews 11:7*

Abraham walked with God

Abraham put his faith in God and had to separate himself from his own country, his father's house, and their ungodly ways. Sarah is also mentioned for her faith and how, being past the age of childbearing had faith to conceive a child.

> *"By faith, Abraham obeyed when he was called to go out to the place which he would receive as an inheritance. And he went out not knowing where he was going." Hebrews 11:8.*

Moses walked with God

Even though Moses had become a prince in Egypt, he chose to obey God and lead His people out of slavery to the promised land.

> *"Choosing rather to suffer affliction with the people of God than to enjoy the passing pleasures of sin...By faith he forsook Egypt, not fearing the wrath of the king; for he endured by seeing Him who is invisible." Hebrews 11:25-27.*

One thing in common

They were declared righteous in their generation and shunned sin by walking in the ways of God and not in the ways of the wicked.

The scripture also states that we are responsible for walking with God and not being contaminated by an ungodly world, just like the examples mentioned.

We have to reach the world with the gospel but keep ourselves from the world's sinful ways.

Walking in the Spirit

As New Testament believers, we read that if we *"Walk in the Spirit, we will not fulfill the lusts of the flesh." Galatians 5:16.* We can tell if we are walking in the Spirit by the fruit of the Spirit in our lives.

> *"The fruit of the Spirit is love, joy, peace, longsuffering, kindness, goodness, faithfulness, gentleness, self-control, against such there is no law." Galatians 5:22-23.*

Nothing can condemn us if we are walking in the Spirit. By walking in the Spirit, may we overcome temptation and the lusts of the flesh.

Day 34 (Journal)

Today is a Saturday. I spent the day with family and some students. I drove a busload to Idlers Bay, a beautiful beach with a fringing coral reef. It is great for snorkeling, though you have to watch out for poisonous sea snakes around the reef. We had a great day.

Chapter 22

Where are the spiritual Fathers?

Day 35 (Journal)

Today is Sunday. Only five days to go!

Luaki Taufau led a fantastic time of worship this morning. Luaki and his wife, Kipi, are ex-students and are now a part of the ministry team.

John Pasterkamp is speaking this morning. John is the pioneering founder and father of CLC in PNG.

John spoke on a fitting subject, 'The Father heart of God'. John is a true father in the faith and is respected, loved, and admired throughout PNG.

Rewind for a moment - The first time I met John, I was an assistant pastor to Hal Oxley in Melbourne. I loved John's gentle spirit and compassion as he shared stories about his pioneering experiences in PNG.

Hal and John arranged for me to do a ministry trip to PNG. I enjoyed that trip to PNG. I got on so well with John that it was as if we had always known one another. I also loved ministering to the people In PNG, as they were open and receptive to the gospel.

When I returned to Melbourne after John had mentioned that he would like to start a Bible College, I could not get the thought out of my mind. I had been lecturing at Life Bible College in Melbourne for several years and loved it.

I formulated a plan for establishing a similar Bible College in PNG. It involved ten significant things that would be needed to start a College. I shared the project and the burden with my wife. She was not overjoyed as we had just moved into a lovely new home we had built in Melbourne. So I said, "Okay, I will put the plan in my study draw, and if God is in it, let Him make the next move."

Some nine months later, Hal and Jill Oxley had gone overseas for a month and left me in charge of opening the church mail. I opened a letter from John Pasterkamp and could not believe what I was reading.

John had sent a letter to Hal saying He felt the Holy Spirit prompted him to write because he believed Hal had someone in his church who could come and establish a Bible College. Then, to my amazement, he listed nine of the ten points I had put in my study draw and said, "Let God make the next move."

It was evident to Hal Oxley and my wife Caroline that God was in it, so we arranged to go and start a College at the beginning of the following year. The rest is history. The College was a great success and had an impact on the nation.

When John returned to Holland many years later, he wrote a book 'Memoirs of the Revival' in the South Pacific. It is a detailed account of John's pioneering spirit and ministry. It is a great read, and I would highly recommend it. It is full of incredible adventures and stories and is one of the most inspirational books I have ever read.

After church - We spent the rest of the day with John and Coby together with some of the ex-students and leaders, Charles and Lucille Lapa, Gabriel and Cecilia Pepson, Edward and Anne Oki, Ango and Lena Wangatau, Luaki and Kipi Taufa, Vagi and Mary Vele, Joe, and Margaret Gabut. We had a great time of fellowship.

Day 36 (Journal)

A lovely day. Took lectures and spoke about church leadership, especially the vital role of Pastors, elders, and deacons in the local church's life.

Inspired by John's message on the 'Father heart of God,' I decided to study more on the subject.

Not many fathers

The Bible tells us that there are not many fathers in the faith. *"For though you might have ten thousand instructors in Christ, yet you do not have many fathers." 1 Corinthians 4:15.*

Many willing instructors want to teach, preach, do bible studies, and proclaim the gospel. But where are the Fathers? There are not many fathers in the faith. Fathers do not have to be old but mature enough to care for people as a father would for his children.

There is a significant lack of national fathers in the church in PNG, but I can see some of these students shaping up to become spiritual fathers.

Fast forward to today, many of them have become spiritual fathers in the faith throughout the nation.

Attributes of Fathers

1. **They act like shepherds** – *"When he saw the multitudes, He was moved with compassion for them, because they were weary and scattered, like sheep having no shepherd." Matthew 9:36-38.*

2. **They are loving and make time for you** – *"So affectionately longing for you, we were well pleased to impart to you not only the gospel of God but also our own lives because you had become dear to us." 1 Thessalonians 1:8.*

3. **They discipline in love and seek to restore** – *"As you know we exhorted, and comforted, and charged every one of you as a father does his own children." 1 Thessalonians 2:11.*

4. **They have faith and are filled with the Spirit** – *"For he was a good man, full of the Holy Spirit and of faith.*

And a great many people were added to the Lord." Acts 11:24.

5. **They desire to take the gospel to the world** – *"This gospel of the kingdom will be preached in all the world as a witness to all nations, and then the end will come." Matthew 24:14.*

Fathers lead by example

Fathers should set an example. Our children watch us and copy us. When our three-year-old son Andrew saw Arthur Blessitt carrying his cross, I had to make a cross for him to carry around. Today, Andrew is now in the ministry as a Baptist pastor. Good fathers will influence others. People will want to follow respected fathers in the faith.

> *"Shepherd the flock of God which is among you, serving as overseers, not by compulsion but willingly, not for dishonest gain but eagerly; nor as being lords over those entrusted to you, but being an example to the flock." 1 Peter 5:2-3.*

I pray that God would raise many more fathers in the faith to disciple, mentor, and lead others.

Hungry For God

Chapter 23

What is the world coming to?

Day 37 (Journal)

In Bible College this morning, my subject was the Second Coming of Christ. After lectures, I took Caroline shopping. I then headed for the hills to pray and study.

I still had this morning's theme of the second coming in my mind. The students were very interested and asked lots of questions.

I thought I would look at Matthew 24 concerning things happening today. When my wife and I hear of wars, murders, and some ways the world is heading, we often say, "What is the world coming to?"

Signs leading to the end of the age

In the first verse of *Matthew 24*, Jesus and the disciples are outside the magnificent temple. The disciples were proud of it because they wanted to show Jesus the incredible structure of the temple.

Jesus did not seem impressed and burst their bubble by saying to them, *"Do you not see all these things? Assuredly, I say to you, not one stone shall be left upon another that shall not be thrown down." Verse 2.*

The disciples must have been shocked, and after thinking about this, asked Jesus three questions,

"Tell us when will these things be? And what will be the sign of Your coming? And of the end of the age? Verse 3.

The theme of Deception

The first sign that Jesus mentions is deception.

"Take heed that no one deceives you." verse 4.

This theme runs throughout this discourse. There will be false Christ's false prophets and false religions. We were shocked when an expatriate family left our church in Port Moresby to join the Bahi faith. Their friends had deceived them.

The roots of deception can be traced back to the first lie in the bible in the Garden of Eden when the devil told Eve an outright lie to deceive her into eating the forbidden fruit.

Jesus called the devil the father of lies. *"....The devil does not stand in the truth because there is no truth in him. When he speaks a lie, he speaks from his own resources, for he is a lie and the father of it." John 8:44*

The devil is cunning, so deception is often close to the truth. Otherwise, we would not be deceived. The devil is on a mission to mislead the whole world if he can.

"So the great dragon was cast out, that serpent of old called the devil and Satan, who deceives the whole world, he was cast to the earth and his angels were cast out with him." Revelation 12:9.

Fast forward to today - We can see an increase in deception through internet scams, mobile phones, and dodgy advertising, often targeting vulnerable people.

Some people are so deceived that they are still unconvinced even when the truth is revealed to them.

The beginning of sorrows (Journal)

Jesus then goes on to list what He calls the beginning of sorrows. It includes wars and rumours of wars, nation against nation, kingdom against kingdom, famines, pestilences, and earthquakes in various places. It appears things will get worse before the return of Christ.

What should we do?

What should we do? Should we stockpile food? Should we arm ourselves? Should we go into hiding? What is the answer? Jesus said, *"See that you are not troubled, for all these things must come to pass, but the end is not yet."* Verse 6.

Jesus gives us the answer; He says, *"See that you are not troubled."* We know these things will happen; we have been forewarned and must put our faith and trust in Christ.

Tribulation and the gospel

All this is followed by betrayal and great tribulation before Christ returns. But the good news is that -

> *"This gospel of the kingdom will be preached in all the world as a witness to all nations, and then the end will come." Verse 14.*

We need to keep proclaiming the gospel no matter what is happening. In these last days, there is only one safe place to be, in Christ and His kingdom.

When is the Kingdom coming?

When the Pharisees asked Jesus when is the Kingdom of God coming? (or the return of Christ). He described what it would be like on Earth at that time. He uses two time periods, the generation of Noah and Lot.

He says it will be like in the days of Noah, *"They ate, they drank, they married wives, they were given in marriage, until the day Noah entered the ark, and the flood came and destroyed them all." Luke 17:26-27.*

Jesus said it would also be like in the days of Lot. *"They ate, they drank, they bought, they sold, they planted, they built; but on the day that Lot went out of Sodom, it rained fire and brimstone and destroyed them all." Luke 17:28-29.*

Both of these generations were caught off guard and unprepared for the judgment that was to come. We can expect many people will be unprepared for the return of Christ when the time comes.

Life back then seemed to be just like now, with people going about their daily business as usual. Why, then, did judgment come on these two generations?

"The Lord saw the wickedness of man was great in the earth, and that every intent of the thoughts of his heart was only evil continually." Genesis 9:5.

"Because the outcry against Sodom and Gomorrah is great, and because their sin is very grave." Genesis 18:20.

The wickedness of man was great because their thoughts were continually evil, and their sin was very grave. What was so grave about the sin of Sodom and Gomorrah that God wanted to destroy the city?

Lot had some men visit him, and the men in the city wanted Lot to send them out so they could have their way with them. Lot offered his daughters, but they preferred the men.

Jesus uses these examples to describe what things will be like around the return of Christ. People will live everyday lifestyles, except people will be evil in their ways. God considered both these generations wicked, and they consequently faced God's judgment.

But the good news is that Noah and Lot both found grace

in the eyes of the Lord and were both saved from the coming judgment.

Because of Christ, we can all find grace in the eyes of the Lord. All we must do is repent of our sins, turn to Christ, and believe in Him for salvation.

Why the delay?

The second coming of Christ has been preached since the days of Jesus and the apostles. All sorts of theories have been put forward as to the unfolding of events and the timing of his return.

I remember some years ago listening to a preacher who had it all worked out using charts to explain the sequence of events. When the planets were lined up in 1982, he implied that that could coincide with the second coming. He was wrong, like so many others.

Many Christians in every generation have become discouraged because of what seems to be a delay in His coming. But the scripture gives us an answer.

*'Scoffers will come in the last days,…..saying, "Where is the promise of His coming?....all things continue as they were from the beginning of creation."…..*The Lord is not slack concerning His promise, not willing that any should perish but that all should come to repentance.'

Because of His mercy and grace, the Lord delays His coming because He wants everyone to have the opportunity to repent and receive Christ as their Saviour and Lord.

Chapter 24
Know your identity in Christ

Day 38 (Journal)

Pastor Bob Lutu is sharing on 'Pastoring a Local Church' with the students this morning. I first met Bob and Ruth when they attended the Bible College I was lecturing at in Melbourne.

They are a lovely couple. Bob returned as the national pastor in Port Moresby but later went to Goroka to pastor the local CLC Church.

Bob is like a teddy bear with an authentic shepherd's heart. He is very compassionate, loving, and wise. Bob has become a father in the faith, and many nationals look to him for wisdom and guidance.

Bob and his wife Ruth were well-loved and respected for their understanding and care for people.

Know who you are

I decided to stay home today to study our identity in Christ. I had become involved in the deliverance ministry, not by choice but necessity, and I needed to reassure myself of my identity in Christ. I was concerned when I read about the incident when Jewish exorcists tried to cast out demons.

> *'Then some of the itinerant Jewish exorcists took it upon themselves to call the name of the Lord Jesus over those who had evil spirits, saying, "We exorcise you by the Jesus whom Paul preaches." Also, there were seven sons of Sceva, a Jewish chief priest, who did so. And the evil spirit answered and said, "Jesus I know and Paul I know; but who are you?" Acts 19:13-15*

The question the demons asked was, "Who are you?" Do you know who you are in Christ? The exorcists did not have a personal relationship with God. They were not born-again believers.

"We exorcise you by the Jesus whom Paul preachers." They had heard about Jesus and tried to cast out demons without having the authority. They were trying to copy Paul and had probably seen other apostles casting out demons.

The result was not pretty; we read, *"Then the man in whom the evil spirit was, leaped on them, overpowered them, and prevailed against them so that they fled out of that house naked and wounded."* Acts 19:16.

The deliverance ministry is not an area to play around with. We should not try and put on a show of power or try and copy others; it just might backfire as it did with them. How embarrassing!

Know you have the authority

Jesus gave his disciples the authority to cast out demons. *"Behold, I give you the authority to trample on serpents and scorpions and over all the power of the enemy, and nothing shall by any means hurt you." Luke 10:19.* The disciples had nothing to fear because they had been given the authority and power to cast out demons and the assurance that nothing could hurt them.

All believers can cast out demons; you do not have to be a recognised ministry.

'And these signs shall follow those who believe. "In My Name, they will cast out demons." Mark 16:16. As a believer, if you have faith to do so, you can cast out demons.

Know your identity

It is good to know your complete identity in Christ. In the next paragraph, you will find scriptures for everything I am about to declare. Here are a few for you to research for yourself.

You are forgiven, born again, a new creation; you are accepted in the beloved; you are complete in Him, a child of God, a joint heir with Jesus. All these and many more I have not mentioned are a part of our identity in Christ.

They are what we inherit by the grace of God. We do not earn these privileges. They have been bestowed on us as believers who declared Jesus the Lord of their lives.

The devil would try and steal our identity by telling us how unworthy we are and that we do not deserve any of this. He tries hard to condemn us. But God has freed us from all of the accusations of the devil to enable us the walk in the power of the Holy Spirit.

Your identity is in Christ, do not let the devil lie to you to steal it from you. Continually remind yourself of your identity in Christ.

Chapter 25

Was it worth it?

Day 39 (Journal)

I only have one day to go. Bob Lutu will continue with lectures today. I will stay home and study. I want to review my journal and evaluate this fasting, prayer, and study time.

What did I learn about fasting?

1. If I can fast and pray for 40 days, anybody can if the Holy Spirit leads them.

2. I had a deep hunger and thirst for God and wanted His direction and guidance.

3. I fasted when I was fit, healthy, and without medical issues. (I lost a lot of weight).

4. I survived on water, fruit juice, a dash of lemonade, and the occasional cup of Milo. (but no food).

5. I lived a normal life, doing what I needed to every day, working, and spending time with family and friends.

What did I learn about prayer?

1. I believe God heard my prayers from the first day. So we do not have to fast and pray for long periods for God to listen to us.

2. I believe prayer is a two-way conversation where we pray, listen for a response, and enter a dialogue with God.

3. It seems that God is more responsive to the prayer of faith and loves to answer, bless us, and bring joy to our hearts.

4. I kept a rough journal of my time in prayer and in the Word. I believe this is a good discipline, and I still try and do it first thing each day.

5. God answers our prayers in his timing and not ours. He knows what is best for us. I know some of my prayers were responded to years later.

What did I learn about studying?

Studying the Word of God has been so faith-building for me. *"Faith comes by hearing, and hearing by the word of God." Romans 10:17.*

Every time I study, I get understanding, revelation, and inspiration from the Word and feel better equipped for ministry.

"All scripture is given by inspiration of God, and is profitable for doctrine, for reproof, for correction, for instruction in righteousness, that the man of God may be complete, thoroughly equipped for every good work. 2 Timothy 3:16-17.

Notice it says all scripture, including the Old Testament. Some pastors seem to shy away from the Old Testament, but we need it to understand the New Testament. Without the old, I could not identify Christ as the Messiah.

We also see that the word helps us verify and understand doctrine, which we need to bring encouragement, correction, and instruction.

I may need to adjust my epistemology -

In light of the above section on 'what did I learn about study,' I feel there are times when I may need to adjust my epistemology to acquire, understand, and interpret knowledge.

What is epistemology? In simple terms, it is the theory of knowledge and deals with how knowledge is gathered and from which source. When I study, I gain knowledge from different resources that help me form an opinion and conclusion. But is it the proper conclusion?

Here is an example of epistemology. My belief that the time is 5:00 p.m. is justified because it is based on the knowledge of the clock. But I know it is true because I walk past at the right moment to justify my belief. We see that what we believe because of our knowledge can also be justifiably true because of the connection with the tangible reality.

The point is that Divine revelation in the word of God is based on knowledge but is justifiably true when the Holy Spirit inspires it, and it becomes a reality in our lives.

For example, I can study the gifts of the Holy Spirit, and it becomes knowledge. But that knowledge becomes a justifiably true reality when I see those gifts manifest and operating according to the knowledge I have gained.

We need good, sound theology and doctrine. Thank God for today's commentaries and knowledge through books, computers, and the preached word.

However, God forbid that we allow our traditional knowledge to block the inspiration and revelation that the Holy Spirit may be trying to impart to us.

I feel challenged during this time to make more room and freedom for the Holy Spirit to help me acquire knowledge, understand it, and explain it realistically.

What did I learn about ministry?

Ministry is a privilege that not everybody has. It is the highest calling we can experience in life. To be assigned to be a pastor to Shepherd the flock of God is a tremendous responsibility. We need to take it seriously and be an example to all.

Others can; You can not!

If you want to be effective in ministry, God will put demands on you that He will not put on other Christians.

'Others can you can not' was the heading of a tract published by the late Leonard Ravenhill. It reads, 'If God has called you to be like Jesus in all your spirit, He will draw you into a life of crucifixion and humility. He will put such demands of obedience on you that you will not be allowed to follow what other Christians do. In many ways, He seems to allow other good people to do things that he will not let you do.

He then quotes, *'If anyone wishes to come after Me, he must deny himself, take up his cross and follow Me. For whoever wishes to save his life will lose it, but whoever loses his life for My sake will find it.' Matthew 16:24-25.*

We must set a standard of excellence that should be an example to all, including our fellow ministers.

Yes, it was worth it

What is the answer to the million-dollar question?

Yes, for me, it was worth it. I would not want to do it again. But it gave me a great sense of achievement that anything is possible once I put my mind to something that I feel God is in.

Is fasting a must?

Do you need to fast and pray for long periods to hear from God? The short answer is "No" unless He is leading you to do so. Our relationship with God is based on grace and faith in what Christ has accomplished through His death on the cross and His resurrection.

We can never earn the right to hear from God because of our works of righteousness, and it is through the imputed righteousness of Christ that has been imparted to us because we believe in Christ as our Saviour and Lord. Therefore, we can hear from God at any time.

I was conscious that I was in tune with God from the first day and probably would have achieved what I sought after a few days.

But I thank God for the experience.

Chapter 26

An amazing last Day

Day 40 (Journal)

Pastor David Muap took the morning lectures.

I drove John Pasterkamp to the airport to leave to return to Holland and Japan. John had been traveling around PNG ministering, and it was great to catch up with him again.

After leaving John, I decided on one last trip up into my secluded spot in the hills, my secret place.

When I got there, all I wanted to do was walk around in the bush, praising and worshipping God and thanking Him for this time, and enabling me to last these 40 days of fasting and prayer.

I was ready for anything

As I walked around, I fully expected some outward manifestation of power from God. I was ready for anything. Maybe angles would show up and give me something to eat. Perhaps the Lord Himself would appear, pat me on the back, and say, "Well done, you good and faithful servant."

I said aloud, "At least reveal your power to me, Lord. Let lightning strike the trees or send an earthquake Lord." Then I yelled, "Where are you, Lord?"

A still, small voice

I will never forget it; I heard him say, ***"Here I am."*** It was a 'still small voice' within me, and I knew it was Him.

I thought of the story of Elijah. The great prophet had fled because his life was in danger. He was hiding in a cave in the mountains, and God told him to stand at the entrance to the cave. Then God displayed incredible power: a strong wind broke rocks into pieces, and there was an earthquake and a fire.

> *But the Lord was not in any of these things, then he heard a 'still small voice,' and God spoke to him (1 Kings 19:11-13).*

A miracle

Rewind for a moment - About a year ago, I had heard this still, small voice before and acted on it, and I knew how powerful it could be. As a church, we had been praying for a baby girl named Saua. It was the first child of a young couple in the church. Her head had begun to swell on one side, and they had taken her to Australia, where scans revealed she had an inoperable tumour in her head and was not expected to live long. We had prayed many times, but nothing changed. One Sunday morning during the service, I heard that still, small voice say within me, "You need to pray for baby Saua, anoint her with oil, and pray for her healing."

I was sitting next to John Pasterkamp, who was about to get up to take communion. I told John what I felt the Lord say to me. John acted immediately and told the congregation what I had just said. You could feel the level of faith rise. John called the couple out with baby Saua. We anointed her with oil and prayed for a miracle. She was healed from that moment onwards. The last time I saw her, she was 20 years of age and living an everyday life. Praise God!

Yes, we seem to want God to do something spectacular, but that still-small voice can also become very powerful when acted upon.

Continuing my review

Almost two years after my time of prayer and fasting and seeking God for future direction, I believe my prayers were answered regarding future ministry. I received an invitation to become the senior pastor of a church back in Lismore, Australia. The church had been through a difficult time as the founder and senior pastor had to be stood down for impropriety.

I flew down to Australia to check it out. It was a great church with excellent facilities. The church was also pioneering a Christian School. I felt God was in it, and some nine months later, as a family, we left PNG and headed for Lismore. We loved our time in Lismore and stayed there for 21 years before I semi-retired and we moved to the Gold Coast.

Our children, by God's grace, all love the Lord and are married and have given us 14 lovely grandchildren. Andrew is an ordained Baptist minister in Brisbane. I thank God for their ongoing stability and attribute much of that to the grace of God and times of intense prayer for them.

A monumental experience

This time of prayer and fasting has been a monumental experience for me. I would never do it again, but it was so precious. It has put me more in tune with the Holy Spirit and enhanced my relationship with God.

Do you have to fast and pray?

Do you have to pray and fast to hear from God? The answer is "No." We are constantly in communion with him. It became apparent when He spoke to me in the first few days about renewing my mind and avoiding becoming double-minded and unstable in all my ways.

These days, I do little, if any, fasting, but by the grace of God, I find He speaks to me as I journal in my quiet times each morning or when I am shaving, in the shower, or driving the car. In other words, when I am not preoccupied with other things on my mind.

I emphasise the grace of God, as I have already started to write a book about my revelation and understanding of God's grace, which liberated me from the bondage of religion.

I hope you have been blessed by reading this book as I have been writing it. Thank you for taking the time to read it.

I hope this book helps put a fire in your belly as you seek God with all your heart. May it inspire you as you hunger and thirst for more of God.

I pray that God will continue to lead you as you journey through life. The Lord bless you and make your life an exhilarating and exciting adventure.

Hungry For God

#1 - Author, after the 40-day fast

#2 - Author and family in PNG

#1 - Group of Bible College students (John Pasterkamp on left, Terry Boyle on right)

#6 - Port Moresby Church crowd

#6 - Traditional welcome after 40 years

In Honour of those now with the Lord

This 40-day fast was some 40 years ago

In loving memory of those that I have mentioned through these chapters who have passed on into Glory at the time of writing this book

Isaac Alipet

Pamela Beaumont

Lenden Butuna

Peter Clyburn

Leka Kema

Bob and Ruth Lutu

Uzziah Movo

David Muap

Johnathan Muap

Mygo

Edward Oki

John and Coby Pasterkamp

Peter and Anne Singut

Kipi Taufau

Vagi Vele

(Please forgive me if I have missed anyone or misspelled names.)

www.ingramcontent.com/pod-product-compliance
Lightning Source LLC
Chambersburg PA
CBHW031252290426
44109CB00012B/540